ENDORSEMENTS

Fr. Bala's book speaks of one of the most challenging undertakings of our life, yet one that is essential for our own wellbeing – the journey towards self-mastery. The author coaches us, in very practical ways, to see within ourselves, to confront the obstacles that hold us back, and to embrace God's grace to conquer the inclinations of our human weaknesses. Throughout, we are encouraged to remain positive and to trust in Christ, with whom everything is possible. In this book, Fr Bala shares his own journey and brings to life many verses in Scripture that offer us insights and encouragement from the word of God. If you are open to the idea of your own journey towards self-mastery, this is the guide for you.

Deacon Bob Evans

Popular Christian author and teacher of Scripture, USA.

Benjamin Bala's moving and inspiring piece speaks of 'self-mastery' as 'self-conquest.' The moral values he encapsulates in his book match the realities of human life. Human beings, by creation and by grace, have been provided with the means to subdue and control creation (cf. Gen. 1: 28-30) beginning with oneself. Thus, the piece is an invaluable guide for all who would wish to embark on the courageous journey to self-mastery.

Sr. Mary Jane Aririguzo, IHM

Canon Law Lecturer

Catholic Institute of West Africa, Port Harcourt, Nigeria

This book of 40 chapters is symbolic. In the Bible, the number 40 is associated with significant landmarks - two contextually cognate ones being the periods of the journey of the Israelites to the Promised Land and Jesus' fast. Each ended in something profound. Navigating through this book is another journey to something profound - a voyage of self-mastery. I have read this book by my mentor, and it has been a strong pillar for me, especially here at Harvard, where it has helped me navigate many otherwise tough moral hills with ease. I recommend it to all who seek life's most important victory - self-conquest. It is a keepsake!

Zakka Junior Emmanuel
Student of Religion, Ethics, and Politics
Harvard Divinity School
Massachusetts, USA

I read through this masterpiece by Fr. Bala at a time when numerous struggles and life challenges plagued me; a time when my choicest reactions to life challenges pulled me down emotionally, and I was left wondering how some people manage life, unperturbed by these similar challenges. With the insights provided herein, I saw the need and practical means of self-improvement, taking back control of myself, and making the best version of myself. In this well-written, practical, and scripturally based book on what self-mastery is and how to begin, progress, and sustain the struggle, I learned a lot, and it has become a handy tool as I continue my journey of self-improvement. I recommend this book to everyone from all spheres of life and all ages. I trust and believe in the efficiency of the help it offers.

Engr. Rosemary Itoro John
Port Harcourt Refinery,
Nigeria

Fr Benjamin Bala takes on the bold subject of “self-mastery”. The book challenges us to tap into our God-given capacity to subdue our weaknesses, tame our excesses, and subject ourselves to the disciplines that guide us toward perfection. He elaborates on the realisation of our need for self-mastery, our capacity to strive for it, and the understanding that God's abundant Grace is available to those determined to struggle. He takes on the subject matter in an easy-to-understand and non-judgmental manner, placing precept upon precept while keeping his audience engrossed in the subject until a firm desire is knotted to put into practice the ideas elaborated in this beautiful piece. If you desire to explore your full potential as designed by God, this book is definitely a sure guide.

Dr Swandy Banta
Public Servant, Emotional Intelligence Scholar,
and Humanitarian Worker,
Jos, Nigeria

The author, Fr. Benjamin Bala, is a Moral Theologian per excellence. In a simple, clear, and lucid manner, he presents one of the most difficult tasks of human enterprise: The Journey Towards

Self-Mastery. The book in your hands is written conversationally and engagingly, inviting readers to participate in their own journey of growth actively. The path to self-mastery, he says, is a process in which we gradually release the mind from all limited ideas, beliefs, paradigms, and assumptions that arise from the material world. He has his own personal stories to show how to achieve this. His use of the Bible and Church teachings proves just how knowledgeable Fr. Benjamin is in his chosen field. This book offers a distinctive framework for addressing this important aspect of human life. It is a must-read.

Fr. Williams Abba, Former Dean of Academics,
St Albert Institute, Fadan Kagoma,
Catholic Diocese of Kafanchan, Nigeria

In this excellent book by the erudite Fr. Benjamin Yakubu Bala, the reader is set to encounter an intellectual masterpiece laced with philosophy anchored in biblical perspectives. Anyone who has ever been in doubt on how to tread the dialectics of self-mastery shall find in Journeying Towards Self-Mastery all the necessary ingredients needed in developing the ideal man. I recommend this book to those committed to crawling out of their uninspiring past and mastering themselves in a world enmeshed in confusion and the pressures of daily living.

MUSA, Simon Reef
Journalist
Columnist, LEADERSHIP Newspapers, Nigeria

Journeying towards Self-Mastery

Benjamin Bala

En Route Books and Media, LLC
Saint Louis, MO

ENROUTE
Make the time

En Route Books and Media, LLC
5705 Rhodes Avenue
St. Louis, MO 63109

Cover credit: Benjamin Bala

ISBN-13: 979-8-88870-442-4
Library of Congress Control Number:
Available at https://catalog.loc.gov

Table of Contents

Chapter 1

NEED FOR SELF-MASTERY

"Do not be conformed to this world, but be transformed by the renewing of your minds, so that you may discern what is the will of God – what is good and acceptable and perfect." (Rom 12:2)

I invite anyone, and all, who seek a deeper understanding of themself as a human person and the wisdom to constructively make use of that understanding to join me in this voyage of self-mastery. This is a journey that involves a struggle one must deliberately undertake. And it is a self-mastery that is quite different from the prevailing meaning of that term.

For many, the term "self-mastery" has come to mean the ability to control one's impulses, desires, and behaviours to be more proficient at one's job and to have more beneficial relationships. The self-mastery that I speak of is for a much higher purpose. It may indeed bring about improvements in one's work life and personal relationships, but these are, at best, just fortunate benefits. They are not the purpose of the undertaking. The self-mastery I speak about here is a journey aimed at bringing out the finest person God created one to be. Attaining a good degree of self-mastery brings about true inner peace and a sense of fulfillment that only God can give in this life.

All of us are moral beings with an inborn hunger for becoming better persons. Our human weaknesses and untamed excesses hold us at our lowest levels and cause rifts between us, other people, and

God. I am a Catholic priest; I hear the hurts and disillusionments in the hearts and minds of many penitents. I am blessed with years of study of the insights and guidance that the Church has gained over the centuries about the nature of mankind, our earthly struggles, and the ultimate purpose of our existence. I also have years of experience in my own struggles in the journey toward self-mastery. This book is my attempt to share my personal experiences in this endeavour with you.

In this first chapter, I strive to establish the need to embark on the thrilling journey towards self-mastery. Since my childhood, I have always desired to be my better self. But it took me quite some time to think about how this could be achieved. Eventually, I realised that it is a journey of life that one must embark on. The ideas in this book are personal reflections on this undertaking. You may be keen to know whether I have attained this self-mastery that I so desire. Well, I know I have experienced some degree of growth. It is a journey I have started, and I am still on it. So, the struggle continues, as the Latin expression has it: *Aluta continua.*

The journey toward self-mastery involves seeking God's direction. Hence, the thoughts in this book are rooted in sacred scriptures and the teachings of the Church that have long stood the test of time. I have also drawn on other modern disciplines in the humanities, which lead to a better understanding of the human person and can help one become one's better self.

This book is not an exercise in preaching but one of companionship. I have structured the book as a series of very short chapters, covering basically one subject at a time, so that you can advance or pause to reflect at a pace that best suits you. Owing to the wide range of life experiences and circumstances, what convinces one person is not so convincing to another. So, read on and progress at your own pace; I am with you.

The book is a personal reflection prompted by two reasons. The first reason is my personal desire to gain self-mastery, as I have already stated. I have therefore decided to put these reflections down as a personal manual in my struggle to attain self-mastery. The second reason is to share these personal reflections in writing, hoping they may help others who also seek self-mastery.

Consistent factors that often run through as the main causes of conflict among relations, friends, acquaintances, and spouses are the overbearing impacts of moral breaches, in the form of aberrant behaviours and/or utterances by some people toward others. Those who have become so accustomed to their aberrant behaviours and/or utterances dish them out spontaneously and would wonder why anyone would see anything wrong with their offensive conduct and/or utterances.

In my personal encounter, in over twenty years of ministering to God's people, I have enjoyed the trust of many, young and old. Among them were those who sought God's counsel through me during confessions and other personal interactive sessions.

One of the things people struggle with is fractured relationships. Listening to the people, I quickly sensed that the obvious reason for the troubled relationships was their overbearing behaviour and speech. Meanwhile, those with overbearing attitudes saw their behaviour as normal and never expected those suffering their excesses to have any problems with it. Hence, it was always strange for them to hear people around them complaining. Surprisingly, however, the same people would not tolerate half of such behaviours and utterances from anyone else.

Our human weaknesses and untamed excesses, due to the wound of original sin, need to be subdued. This enterprise is a moral burden on each human being, especially Christians, whom Jesus calls upon to be perfect as their heavenly Father (Matt. 5:48). Unfortunately, some people have either tried to appropriate as part of their nature or have given in to sympathy, feeling defeated by their weaknesses and untamed excesses. Hence, most of the time, upon defaulting, such people expend all their energy arguing to justify their actions, with utter insensitivity to how others feel. If no one succumbs to their self-justification, such persons conclude that people do not like them or are delighted in antagonising them. On their part, some of the relations, friends, acquaintances, and spouses of such people are sometimes quick to conclude that such people are selfish. Such conclusions may be bulky and simplistic, and a poor diagnosis of the problem.

In my interactions with these people, I discovered that a good number of them were not helped to address their weaknesses and curb their excesses in their formative years. Some of the excesses were overlooked, allowed to fester, or even pampered by parents who probably did not realise the need to help their children and wards curb them.

Human behaviours are supposed to be guided by the moral principles of right and wrong, moderation and consideration for others. It therefore amounts to excesses when a person consistently acts in total disregard for these principles. The person finds himself offending those around him, leading to avoidable clashes. The cure for this is to engage in a struggle to conquer those weaknesses and untamed excesses instead of insisting on defending one's aberrant behaviours and utterances resulting from them.

Aberrant behaviours and utterances flowing from one's weaknesses and untamed excesses are different from mistakes. A person who makes a mistake due to human limitations feels sorry for it, seeks forgiveness, and makes amends. But an excessive person sees nothing wrong with aberrant behaviour or utterances because such behaviour and utterances have become a normal part of their life. Instead, the person tries to justify themselves, even when it is glaringly obvious to everyone else that the behaviour is wrong.

Interestingly, God made each human being with the capacity to subdue their weaknesses, tame their excesses, and bring them under their control. This is a struggle one must deliberately undertake. There are three very important things one needs to realise in this endeavour. First is the realisation of one's need for self-mastery. Second is the realisation of the God-given capacity in each person to attain self-mastery. Third is the realisation that God's grace readily awaits anyone desirous of embarking on this struggle.

Self-mastery means self-government. It is the subduing of one's weaknesses, the taming of one's excesses, and the gaining of control over them. It is the foundation of a strong, godly life, of growth and human maturity. A person who attains a good degree of self-mastery behaves in an orderly manner, soberly, seriously minded, sane, exhibits sound-mindedness, is discreet, self-disciplined, prudent, moderate, humble, sensitive to other people, and refined. A person who has attained self-mastery is even-minded and does not live an extreme life. He can have a good relationship with God and with fellow men and women.[1]

Parents are the first motivators in a person's journey towards self-mastery. They lay the foundation of the sense of right and wrong in the child. This process begins at birth and, upon reaching the age of reason, the individual gradually assumes responsibility.

Christians have a greater demand to struggle towards the attainment of self-mastery. This is so because at Baptism, a Christian begins a new phase of life as one who Christ redeems. People who have significantly overcome their weaknesses and curbed excesses are happier and more refined in their behaviour and speech. Getting to that state is not by accident but the result of a struggle in response to our Lord's call to perfection. This is the challenge put forward by this book.

---

[1] John W. Ritenbaugh, "What the Bible Says About Self Mastery". https://bibletools.org/index.cfm/fuseaction/Topical.show/RTD/cgg/ID/136Self-Mastery.htm.

Chapter 2

YOU MUST BE PERFECT

"You, therefore, must be perfect as your heavenly Father is perfect." (Matt. 5:48).

The Christian who struggles to attain self-mastery invariably struggles to attain perfection. In fact, perfection is the object of self-mastery. The Greek word for perfect is *teleios.* It is the adjectival form of the noun *telos,* meaning an end, a purpose, an aim, a goal,[1] etc. When a thing has realised the full purpose for which it was planned, designed, and made, it is said to be *teleios* - perfect. Hence, one is perfect if one has realised the purpose for which God created and sent one into the world. One who is fully grown in stature is *teleios* in contradistinction to a growing person. To be perfect, therefore, means to attain consummate human integrity and virtue, to become full-grown, to attain full maturity. It means to attain maturity in character. In Old Testament thinking, to be perfect means to be without blemish, as in the case of an animal that is considered fit for sacrifice. Jesus demands that each of his followers be perfect. To be perfect, therefore, is a call to become like God.[2] This is the bedrock for the call to Christian morality and the journey towards self-mastery.

---

[1] BibleWorks.

[2] William Barclay, "The Gospel of Matthew Volume 1". *The Daily Study Bible.* Bangalore: Theological, 1999. Pp. 176-8.

The auxiliary verb "must" makes the demand "to be perfect" an imperative. In other words, it is not optional but binding on every follower of Christ. The struggle for perfection does not accommodate excuses or the shifting of blame. It is a struggle that is to be concerted. The demand for perfection becomes binding on each Christian from the day of baptism. It places the challenge on each Christian to struggle towards the goal for which God created us – to become like Him. This struggle entails an effort to conquer our weaknesses and untamed excesses.[3] A person's level or degree of progress towards perfection shows the degree of self-mastery the person has attained.

Interestingly, this demand comes at the end of the Lord's teaching on certain weaknesses and untamed excesses manifest in the aberrant tendencies and habits which his followers must fight against. These are: brooding anger (Matt. 5:21-26), lust (27-30), divorce (31-32), the breaking of vows (33-37), the desire to take revenge (38-42), hatred for enemies (43-47). The call to be perfect by our Lord is a call to struggle to overcome these untamed excesses.

It was the ancient philosopher, Socrates, who once said that an unexamined life is not worth living. The struggle to be perfect is a journey that requires periodic assessment of one's progress. And for the assessment to be fruitful, one must own up to one's inadequacies. The purpose of the assessment is to evaluate and determine the level of progress one is making in subduing one's weaknesses and untamed excesses. The evaluation also offers the Chris-

---

[3] CCC, no. 2013.

tian the opportunity to strategise and to see the areas of life that they may need to give more attention to. In this evaluation, the Christian must be in touch with their innermost self and face the reality of their life with honesty. Moments of meditation, personal prayers, and retreats offer ample opportunities for such.

The Christian must not be afraid to go into their innermost self because that is where one dialogues with oneself and one's Creator. One must not give in to discouragement over failures and fluctuations in the struggle. The determination to make progress in the journey towards perfection should be the spur. As with every other struggle, one must always rise and continue after a fall. Christians need to realise that the path to righteousness is not smooth. It sometimes has rough spots on which the righteous may stumble and fall, but must always rise and continue. The Scriptures speak when they say that "A righteous man [and woman] may fall seven times" (Prov. 24:16).

On the journey towards perfection, the Christian must constantly fix their eyes on Christ under the reasonable guidance of a pastor. These are fellow Christians and co-partners on the journey towards perfection to whom God has entrusted a special responsibility of leading and guiding His people. This is succinctly expressed by St. Augustine of Hippo: "For you I am a bishop; but with you, I am a Christian".[4] The golden fact is that each of them is also struggling towards perfection. They indeed have a challenge to lead by example because to them, much has been given (Luke 12:48). However, our focus must not be on them but on Christ. In

---

[4] "St. Augustine of Hippo", https://catholicdos.org.

the next chapter, we shall see that in attaining self-mastery, a person attains self-conquest and gains control over oneself.

Chapter 3

SELF-CONQUEST

"A man without self-control is like a country broken and left without walls". (Prov. 25:28)

There is an old saying that "A man who conquers himself is greater than one who conquers a thousand men in battle" (Buddha). To attain self-mastery, one must conquer oneself. One who has conquered oneself has captured and taken control over one's weaknesses and untamed excesses. Such a person can exercise self-control. A person who has no self-mastery unarguably has no self-control. The Holy Bible says that "A man without self-control is like a country broken and left without walls" (Prov. 25:28). Also, it says that "He who is slow to anger is better than the mighty, and he who rules his spirit than he who takes a city" (Prov. 16:32).

There are modern theories across disciplines that attribute the display of unguarded, unredeemed tempers, ill feelings, and intolerance towards others to traits such as temperament and other determinants. These theories present these traits as inherent behavioural programming factors in human beings that constrain them and render them incapable of positive behavioural change. This is an oversimplified vindication aimed at shifting responsibility for personal actions. Such theories make a person feel incapacitated from pursuing positive change, leading to surrender to these factors and a failure to take full responsibility for one's actions. The theories contradict the nature of human beings created in freedom and the place of God's grace, which assists the Christian in the struggle towards perfection. They make the human being fixed and behaviourally deterministic, resulting in behavioural stagnation and making a person comfortable with their lower self. Pope Francis refers to these new theories as "contemporary Gnosticism," which presumes "a subjective faith whose only interest is a certain experience or set of ideals and bits of information which are meant to console and enlighten, but which ultimately keep one imprisoned in his or her own thoughts and feelings".[1]

The creator made us free and responsible. This is clear from the creation account: "And the Lord God commanded the man, saying, 'You may freely eat of every tree of the garden; but of the tree of the knowledge of good and evil you shall not eat, for in the day that you eat of it you shall die'" (Gen. 2:16-17). This shows that God did not make us with behavioural programming that limits our capacity to change for the better. Were it so, it would have been unjust for God to hold us responsible for our actions - good or bad. This would have also rendered invalid the challenge for the Christian to struggle towards being perfect as his heavenly Father is perfect (Matt. 5:48). Besides, Jesus would not have bothered himself with providing answers to the question of "What must I do?" (Matt. 19: 16; Mark 10:17; Luke 18:18).

Christians must not give in to vindicating theories which make them behaviourally deterministic. Instead, they are to recognise their human imperfections, which manifest in their weaknesses and untamed excesses, and undertake a serious struggle to conquer

---

[1] Pope Francis, *Gaudete et Exsultate.* No. 36.

them. Christians are to rely on God's grace, which accompanies them in their struggle to conquer themselves (2 Cor. 12:9), through the action of the Holy Spirit, who is our ever-willing helper. Christians must quit theories that vindicate persons of responsibility for inadequacies and untamed excesses. This has resulted in the stagnation of many behaviours. A Christian is to engage in a very serious struggle to conquer the self. Plato, the great philosopher, is quoted to have said that the first and best victory is to conquer self, since to be conquered by self is, of all things, the most shameful and objectionable.

The struggle towards self-mastery requires personal effort. It involves the determination to put in the struggle to conquer oneself. This determination must flow from a conscious act of reflection that leads one to feel discomfort with one's present state of the lower self. What follows is the conviction that the struggle must begin. A person needs a strong will and perseverance in this struggle. Conquering oneself requires a person to target the very person God created him to be. In the Holy Bible, God made man in his image and likeness (Gen. 1:27). That is our very nature and essence. Our behaviours must therefore mirror that image and likeness of God. The Christian is not to be comfortable with any behaviour that is below his status and dignity.

The sin of our first parents, also called the fall, left a wound on each human being called concupiscence. This wound brought humanity down to a lower level because we lost our original state of being. But God sent his Son to lift us up and restore us to our original state of being, only a little less than God (Psalm 8:5). Jesus made us adopted sons of God, a status to which he charges us to conform our conduct. This is where the serious effort at self-conquest to attain self-mastery comes in. But what exactly is the essence of self-mastery? The next chapter provides the answer to this question.

Chapter 4

ESSENCE OF SELF-MASTERY

"I die every day." (1 Cor. 15:31)

The original sin, the sin of our first parents, Adam and Eve, which each human being inherited, left a damning consequence on humanity, which is the loss of original holiness[1]. The original personal harmony by which the spiritual soul faculties of a person exercised control over one's body got shattered; the relationship between man and woman became subject to tensions, as a result of which their relationship became marked by lust and the tussle for domination; the harmony between humans and creation got broken; death came into the equation of human life.[2]

The injury dealt to our human nature by original sin leaves us with weaknesses and excesses manifesting in aberrant tendencies and habits, which each Christian must struggle daily to conquer. St. Paul refers to this injury of original sin as what constitutes the old self in us, which we must put off and clothe ourselves with a new self (Eph. 4:22-23). He himself lived his Christian life struggling to conquer his old self. He told the Corinthians, "I die every day" (1 Cor. 15:31). He refers to these weaknesses and untamed excesses as deeds of the body and admonished the Romans to destroy them by putting them to death so that they might live. This is exactly the essence of self-mastery; it is a struggle to put to death one's old self.

---

[1] CCC, no. 399.

[2] CCC, no. 400.

When a Christian allows human weaknesses and untamed excesses to grow and fester, they will be in control of one's life to the extent that the one sees nothing wrong with their actions. In this situation, the person is said to be conquered by the person's self. Self-mastery is a daily struggle aimed at liberating the individual from the clutches of one's weaknesses and untamed excesses. The more gains a Christian makes in conquering them, the more they move towards perfection. This is a journey of life that begins at baptism.[3] When the Christian is buried with Christ and raised to newness of life with him (Rom. 6:1-23), by baptism, we are reborn. Original sin and our personal sins are washed away, we are purified and made new creatures, and we become incorporated into the Church, which is the body of Christ.[4] This journey is part of the package that comes with the fundamental option to be a follower of Christ.

In daily Christian living, Christians find themselves amid different voices and ideologies that are often at odds with the demands of following Christ. Those ideologies actually fan the flames of human weaknesses and untamed excesses. Interestingly, some of the proponents of these ideologies craftily use selective portions of the bible, mostly out of context, to give credence to their theories. Unfortunately, some Christians, especially those with a flair for new things, buy into these theories. The result is that the Christian finds himself struggling with two conflicting ideologies.

This explains why it is common today to see people who profess a certain depth of Christian faith, while their weaknesses and

---

[3] CCC, no. 2342.

[4] CCC, no. 1262-1270.

untamed excesses flourish and have a strong hold on their lives. Some virtually celebrate their flaws so that when accosted, they proudly say to you, "This is me" or "This is who I am". The question is, can that be said to be the real "who" of the person? This question is dealt with in chapter seven. The struggle to attain self-mastery redirects a person who may have deviated back to his real self. It connects the person to the two poles of his existence: his origin and destination. By self-mastery, we realise our own essence and the essence of our existence on earth. Without attaining self-mastery, we are far from our essence.

Self-mastery is not attained only by a series of prayers and fasting, attending retreats, revivals, and crusades, night vigils, etc. If this were so, most Christians would have attained the crescendo of self-mastery. But it requires a personal struggle, which many often relegate to the back seat. The Christian must, in addition to these spiritual commitments, make deliberate and concerted efforts to conquer himself or herself. Jesus tells us that his true followers and children of his Father's kingdom are not those who only say Lord, Lord, but those who also do the will of his Father (Matt. 7:21). At this point, the question to ask is, do humans actually have what it takes to attain the noble moral desire of self-mastery? Do humans have the faculty for self-subduing and bringing their excesses under control and conquering themselves? This is the focus of the next chapter.

Chapter 5

SUBDUING FACULTY

"A fool takes no pleasure in understanding.
but only in expressing personal opinion." (Prov. 18:2)

The faculty that is instrumental in the subduing of our weaknesses and untamed excesses is our rational faculty, supported by strong willpower. The rational faculty means the ability to think. It is also referred to as reasoning. Our rational faculty is the instrument of self-control in each human being. It is in the rational faculty that every individual processes their actions. The evaluation of the rightness or wrongness of the action, the decision, and the actual choice of the action takes place in man's rational faculty. Here, we are talking about voluntary actions, called "human acts," that a person can control.

There is a difference between human acts and acts of man. A human act has two elements. First, the person knows the action, including whether it is right or wrong. Second, the person acts on his own free will, i.e., without coercion, e.g., talking, driving, walking, etc. An act of man, i.e., an involuntary act, is an action which does not proceed from knowledge and free will, e.g., breathing, eye blinking, yawning, dreaming, etc.

God blessed human beings with a rational faculty from creation. We are rational by our very nature; that is why we are Homo sapiens. The rationality faculty consists of the human intellect. It is on this rationality that God entrusted the dominion of the earth to man (Gen. 1:28). According to St. Thomas Aquinas, rationality is what makes a human being intelligent, and this rationality resides in the human soul, which acquires knowledge of truth through reason.[1] And reasoning is the practical working of the intellect.[2] Therefore, God intended that every action of ours should proceed from reasoning.

Closely related to the rational faculty is God's gift of free will. Free will is "...the act of the will making a free choice".[3] Free will operates in the light of knowledge as the intellect furnishes it.[4] By free will, a person independently chooses to do whatever the person wants to do, right or wrong (Gen. 2:16-17). By the endowment of human beings with the gift of free will, God chose not to make them robots to be remotely controlled by him. God did this to enable human beings to take full responsibility for their actions. Human beings make their choices freely, act freely, and are free to change the course of their actions at any time. This is why Aquinas says that "God made man in the beginning and left him free to make his own decisions".[5] Therefore, when one has exercised one's free will and carried out an action, one must take responsibility.

Our rational faculty works just like our digestive system. When we eat food, the body processes it, uses what is useful to nourish our tissues, and excretes what is not. Similarly, our rational faculty

---

[1] Thomas Aquinas, *Summa Theologiae: A Concise Translation.* McDermott, Timothy (Ed.). Notre Dame: Christian Classics, 1989. p. 98.

[2] Paul J. Glenn, *A Tour of the Summa of St. Thomas Aquinas.* Bangalore: Theological, 2007. p. 65.

[3] Glenn, p. 69.

[4] Ibid.

[5] Thomas Aquinas, *Summa Theologiae.* p. 128.

digests every thought that our minds conceive in a discursive process, weighs and considers the course of the action and its pros and cons; right or wrong, fitting or unfitting, convenient or inconvenient, proper or improper, civil or uncivil, polite or rude, sensitive or insensitive, etc. We are to put into action only what is fine and good for human consumption and to throw away whatever is not good for human consumption.

In functioning as a sensor mechanism and as a digestive system, our rational faculty guards all our actions arising from our weaknesses and untamed excesses. This is how the rational faculty serves as a subduing faculty. Each person must take ownership of his rational capacity and put it to use in his struggle to attain self-mastery. Human actions should not be guided by instincts, as those of animals. The only justifiable instinctive action is that of self-preservation. If at any point one acts without fully engaging one's rational faculty, then one has acted below one's God-given nature. To ignore the rational faculty and act according to what one feels is dangerous because it leads to arbitrariness, which is counterproductive to the attainment of self-mastery. Therefore, each person needs to make full use of their subduing faculty. The subduing faculty is the faculty responsible for the choices as one exercises one's freedom. The next chapter picks up on this topic.

Chapter 6

FREE BUT LIABLE

"See, I have set before you today life and prosperity, death and adversity."
(Deut. 30:15)

Discoveries in modern psychology have helped improve understanding of the human person and their behavioural patterns. However, not every theory in human psychology aligns with Christian tenets. Some of them are deterministic, thereby contradicting the Christian understanding of freedom and responsibility. Some of these modern determinist theories have tried to explain away the pervasive grip of human weaknesses and untamed excesses that manifest in aberrant habits. Such theories have attributed the erratic behaviours and displays of unguarded tempers and intolerance to certain traits, such as temperaments and other factors like dates of birth,[1] etc., thereby legitimising and fanning them into flames. The impression is that these traits are inherent behavioural programming factors that inhibit the human will, constrain the person, and condemn them to act as they do.

Theories such as these, try to impress on the human mind that human behaviours, including those arising from their weaknesses and untamed excesses, are conditioned by certain behaviour-controlling traits. Those who settle for these theories eventually get caught in a defeatist web, feeling helpless in the face of their weaknesses and untamed. If humans were created as these theories try

[1] https://www.dgreetings.com. 10.01.2019.

to impress on people, then our Lord's call for perfection would have made no sense. Such deterministic theories contradict the Christian understanding of human nature, created in freedom by God. The theories also disregard the place of God's grace, which assists the Christian in the struggle towards perfection. The theories make a person feel comfortable with his lower self and "keep one imprisoned in his or her own thoughts and feelings".[2]

Holy Scriptures reveal that God created human beings free and responsible. These two attributes of man make him liable for his actions as expressed by God: "You may freely eat of every tree of the garden; but of the tree of the knowledge of good and evil you shall not eat, for in the day that you eat of it you shall die" (Gen 2:16-17). The dialogue, leading to the eventual decision to eat of the fruits of the tree, is a practical manifestation of the exercise of that freedom (Gen 3:1-6). The choice between life and death (Deut 30:15) is a pointer to the freedom God gave to humans. Jesus respected the freedom of his followers who chose to leave him (Jn 6:66). He even asked the disciples to decide whether to stay with him or go away (v. 67).

Worth emphasising here is that God did not make human beings with behavioural programming that gags and limits their capacities for decision-making and action, whether good or bad. Were it so, it would have been unjust for God to hold us responsible for our actions. His punishing of Adam and Eve would have been unjust (Gen 3:14-19). This would have also rendered invalid the challenge for the Christian to struggle towards being perfect

---

[2] Pope Francis, *Gaudete et Exsultate.* No. 36.

(Mt 5:48). Similarly, Jesus would not have bothered himself with providing answers to the question, "What must I do?" (Mt 19:16; Mk 10:17; Lk 18:18). He would have probably responded, "Go and respond as your traits drag you". So, freedom is essential in the struggle to attain self-mastery.

Church moral theology teaches that "Freedom is the power rooted in reason and will, to act or not to act, to do this or that, and so to perform deliberate actions on one's own responsibility.[3] It is important to note that freedom does not consist in the right to say or do just anything. Freedom is meant to be exercised with due consideration for the good of those around, so that a person does not pursue his own selfish interests to the detriment of others. Freedom must be exercised in justice and charity. Otherwise, one deviates from the moral law and violates one's own freedom.[4] This means that human freedom is limited and fallible.[5] The freedom of the other people around limits it. That is why it must be exercised in relation to other people.[6]

Freedom is the basis for which a person can be praised when he has done good or blamed when he has done wrong. It is the basis for rewarding good deeds and for punishing bad deeds.[7] Freedom makes a person responsible for one's actions as long as the person acted voluntarily.[8] Determinist theories compromise this sense of

---

[3] CCC, no. 1731.

[4] CCC, no. 1740.

[5] CCC, no. 1739.

[6] CCC, no. 1738.

[7] CCC, no. 1732.

[8] CCC, no. 1734.

responsibility of human freedom to a very large extent, thereby making man a casualty of his own very freedom. They mislead one into overshooting the limits of one's freedom and eventually making oneself a slave to one's own freedom.

Christian moral thoughts, therefore, understand a human as one created by God with the capacity to tame and conquer one's weaknesses and untamed excesses through the act of self-mastery. In other words, all the biological traits in humans are subject to each person's will, where the person freely decides to act or not to act, to do good or to do bad. God did not put the human will under the control of any biological traits in the person. Even though they exert a strong influence on the intellect and will and can sway a person's analysis of an act, the will still has the upper hand at the moment of decision.

Christians must therefore not give in to deceptive vindicating extremist theories which make them behaviourally deterministic and divorced from the culpability of their actions. Instead, they are to recognise their human imperfections, which manifest in their weaknesses and untamed excesses, and undertake a serious struggle to conquer them. Theories that conceive a human being without freedom and responsibility do injury to the very essence and nature of man created by God. The Christian must decide and be determined to struggle to gain mastery of self. But this requires the Christian to take total ownership of their life and not to give in to misleading theories.

One's level of self-mastery shows one's level of human development. A person who has made advancements in age, physical growth, and academic achievement without a corresponding growth in self-mastery is a contradiction. A Christian must translate their knowledge into concrete action. And when a person fails to meet up, the person should take full responsibility, make amends, and improve. It is contradictory for a person to accept accolades for good actions but shift responsibility by invoking deterministic theories as excuses. Such deterministic theories include claims like "This is who I am." The next chapter discusses the question of who we are in perspective.

Chapter 7

WHO IS THIS ME?

"So, God created mankind in his image, in the image of God he created them." (Gen. 1:27)

There are times when we see a person act insensitively towards others. The person displays a behaviour that blatantly offends the sensitivity of others; a behaviour that is clearly below the standards of modest expectations - a purely egocentric behaviour. We see people who speak or act in very rash ways. When questioned, we hear such a person put on defences like: "This is me; that is who I am." You hear some confessing that they cannot change who they are. This attitude is a common occurrence even among some Christians. This kind of position is fuelled by self-centred, deterministic philosophies of life, as already noted in chapter six. Arrogant claims such as these raise serious questions. What then do such people mean when they say, "this is me" or "that is who I am"?

The assertion, "This is me" or "That is who I am" by such aberrant people is a declaration by them meaning, "This is my nature", "This is the way I have been created", "This is who I am". By implication, the person is saying that it is in his essential nature to act as he does, and that he has the right to behave so. It means nature has predetermined the person's actions. Therefore, he feels comfortable with his aberrant acts and should not be blamed because he has acted according to how nature has programmed him. The person feels momentary satisfaction because the action has satisfied his immediate desire. Clearly, the assertion "This is me" in this case is a denial of the real "who" that the person is. The big question, then, is: who is the real me?

Christian anthropology traces the nature of each person back to the creation of mankind. It reveals two important facts about the nature of the human being. First, God made mankind in his image and likeness (Gen 1:27) in a state of holiness.[1] Second, God made mankind free and responsible (Gen 2:16-17).[2] Mankind misused God's given freedom, disobeyed God's command and sinned (Gen. 3: 1-7) and lost the grace of his original holiness.[3] From this moment, weaknesses wounded man's nature and his untamed excesses, which manifest in aberrant behaviours. However, God did not abandon mankind to the power of sin[4] but redeemed mankind through Jesus Christ (Eph. 1:3-7; Col. 1:19-20).

Our true nature, therefore, is that we are the image and likeness of God and redeemed by Christ.[5] This is the real "You" that every Christian is. And this is the status the Christian is to live in accordance with, a child of God who has become salt of the earth and light of the world (Matt. 5:13-16). And to be salt and light, the Christian must conquer and subdue his weaknesses and untamed excesses inflicted on him by original sin. Christ sets standards for his followers by challenging them to a life of perfection (Matt. 5:20-

---

[1] CCC, no. 338.

[2] CCC, no. 396.

[3] CCC, no. 399.

[4] CCC, no. 410.

[5] https://www.usccb.org 21.01.2019. see Eucharistic Prayer IV.

48). He tells the rich young man to keep the commandments (Mark 10:19) and to be sensitive to the hungry poor by selling his possessions and giving the money to them (Mark 10:21).

Following the footsteps of the master, St. Paul admonishes the Christian not to conform to the world. He has been transformed into doing only what God wills (Rom. 12: 2). He is to put aside disobedience, anger, wrath, malice, slander, violence, and abusive speech, etc. (Col. 3:6-8). Peter urges the Christian to break from a life ruled by his passions, debauchery, drinking to excess, having wild parties, drunken orgies (1 Peter 4:3). These are all manifestations of weaknesses of the fallen man and untamed excesses which the child of God must struggle to conquer and subdue and attain self-mastery.

This, therefore, means that a Christian who exhibits such weakness of a fallen nature and untamed excesses, and at the same time arrogantly claims, "that is who I am," disclaims the image and likeness of God that he is. He also disclaims his redeemed nature. It is a brazen contradiction for a Christian whom Christ has washed in the waters of baptism to lay such a claim. Christians must, hence, be careful not to disclaim who they are and claim a deceptive nature. Perhaps it is good to clarify that we have no choice in who we are, but we have a choice in what we become. Self-mastery is an endeavour that takes us back to who we are, i.e., the "who" that God created us to be.

God created human beings with the seed of growth and development. At conception, a person becomes a tiny, unrecognised figure in the womb and grows into an embryo. In the ninth month, the person is normally born as a fragile baby. He then grows and matures, encompassing different aspects of life: intellectual, moral, social, psychological, spiritual, etc. At baptism, the new life of Christ is planted in the Christian, who is expected to nurture it to a maturity called perfection, also known as self-mastery. A Christian with a “that is who I am” mindset has simply boxed himself into a small prison of contentment, which closes the windows of possibilities for growth and development. Such a mindset is a grave obstacle on the journey towards self-mastery.

Chapter 8

YOU HAVE A CHOICE

"To act faithfully is a matter of your own choice." (Sirach 15:15)

Every day of our lives, we face choices. This is an opportunity God gave human beings to exercise their gift of freedom. Of all creatures of God, only human beings can make choices because they are endowed with intellect, which is later treated as the subduing faculty. No one escapes the reality of making choices, since not choosing is itself a choice. Each choice has an opportunity cost; there is always something one must give up.[1] However, Ben Sira makes it clear that every choice entails responsibility, which is why God judges each person according to his deeds.[2]

Our lives and particularly our journey towards self-mastery involve choices. It is very important to understand this, since some Christians believe that God does everything and is responsible for all that happens to them in life. They go so far as to attribute their aberrant behaviours and the negative consequences of those behaviours to God. Some have made a doctrine out of this dangerous mentality so that even when they have done wrong, they believe that it was God who made it so.

---

[1] Evaristus Nnamene, Make Your Choice. (Homily delivered at the St. John the Baptist Chaplaincy, CIWA, Obehie), early February 2020.

[2] Daniel J. Harrington, "Sirach" (15:11-20). The International Bible Commentary: An Ecumenical Commentary For The Twenty-First Century (Bangalore: Theological, 2007) P. 998

The author of the book of Sirach, Ben Sira, vehemently objects to any suggestion of God making it possible for people to do wrong. He insists on the fundamental incompatibility between the all-wise God and the wrong conduct of human beings. He emphasises human freedom in the face of right and wrong. God considered his gift of freedom to human beings so important that even after our first parents abused it and fell into sin, God did not take it away. This freedom refers to a person's internal disposition to choose between right and wrong. God never interferes with our freedom.[3]

We can talk of two types of choices. The first is the choice between what is good and what is evil/bad. This kind of choice is straightforward. One has only to choose between two clear options. The second is the choice between two or more good things. In this situation, the person is guided by the options for what is better or best to do in any given circumstances. Here, wisdom should guide the person to choose the better of two options or the best of three or more.

Making decisions is part of the natural rhythm of human life and is inevitable in the journey towards self-mastery. A Christian who wants to attain self-mastery must realise this and take full responsibility. The person need not, by any means, push this duty to God. Nothing can change God's decision to take decision-making power from a person, given the precious gift of freedom he gave humans. Besides, those who believe they can use prayer as a tool to remote control God hold a belief which is in direct opposition to

---

[3] Ibid.

the sovereignty of God's Will. However, in answer to a person's prayers, God can grant them grace and wisdom for discernment in the choices before them. But the individual must finally make the choice. Christians who shift the burden of decision-making in their lives to God and attribute the choices of their actions to God lie to themselves and will never make significant progress in the journey towards self-mastery.

The art of decision-making is a duty for every adult. Coming to terms with the reality of an individual's obligation is a mark of wisdom and maturity. This means the person is taking responsibility for their life and the daily fallout of their weaknesses and untamed excesses. In this way, the person can take responsibility for the consequences of their actions.[4] People like this neither blame anyone, including God, for their actions nor the eventual negative consequences of their wrong choices, nor do they excuse themselves. Hardy discusses a fundamental shift each successful person must make upon reaching adulthood. That shift is the decision to take responsibility for one's actions.[5] With this shift, one puts oneself on the path to happiness and takes control of one's life, which is necessary on the journey towards self-mastery. A genuine shift entails putting the past behind and facing the future with hope.

---

[4] https://www.mindtools.com.

[5] Benjamin P. Hardy, "The Two Mental Shifts Highly Successful People Make". https://www.qz.com.

Chapter 9

OLD THINGS MUST ALWAYS GIVE WAY

"If anyone is in Christ, there is a new creation: everything old has passed away."
(2 Cor. 5:17)

One of the reasons it is difficult for Christians to conquer and subdue their weaknesses and untamed excesses is the inability to disconnect from their old ways. In the life of anyone, especially a Christian, on the journey towards self-mastery, "old things must always give way". The designation "old things" here refers to one's old behaviours that are clear manifestations of one's weaknesses and untamed excesses.

Baptism is the basis of the whole Christian life and the gateway to life in the Holy Spirit.[1] Through baptism, every Christian is freed from sin and its consequences, and reborn as a son or daughter of God, made in the image of Christ, and incorporated into the church[2] as full members of the new kingdom of God, the Christian is regenerated into a new creation because they are buried and raised with Christ in baptism.

By this act of regeneration, the Christian becomes a 'partaker of the divine nature of Christ'. The Christian becomes a member of Christ and a co-heir with him and his body, the temple of the Holy Spirit.[3] Baptism elevates the Christian above their fallen state to a

---

[1] CCC, no. 1213.

[2] CCC, no. 1213.

[3] CCC, no. 1265.

state of redemption. This elevation marks the Christian's departure from old to new ways of life (2 Cor. 5:17). Baptism marks that turning point. It positions the Christian on a journey towards perfection, which involves conquering and subduing their weaknesses and untamed excesses.

Even though Christians, after baptism, still carry the wounds of the old self, they are now endowed with sanctifying grace, which gives them the ability and power to live a life of virtue.[4] Sanctifying grace gives the Christian will the strength to exercise control over their weaknesses and untamed excesses. Sanctifying grace better positions Christians to live according to the demands and principles of the new state.

Jesus calls his followers to a radical departure from their former ways of life, even in the practice of the Mosaic Law. He states in the indicator phrase, "You have heard how it was said" (Matt. 5:21-47). This indicator phrase suggests a shift, the introduction of new expectations. Hence, members of his new kingdom are liable to judgement not only for killing but also for anger that nurses revenge. They are guilty of adultery even by looking at a woman lustfully. They are to love not only those who love them but also those who hate them. This radical departure is perhaps more categorically expressed by Jesus in his warning on the danger of putting new wine in old wineskins: "No one puts new wine in old wineskins; if he does, the wine will burst the skins, and the wine is lost, and so are the skins; but fresh wine is for fresh skins" (Mk 2:22). Self-

---

[4] CCC, no. 1266.

mastery requires the concrete actualisation of this departure by the Christian in his actions.

Therefore, Christians who continue to act comfortably in their old ways, in their weaknesses and untamed excesses, manifesting aberrant behaviours, have yet to make concrete that radical Christian departure. This radical departure is not only necessary; it is the starting point in the struggle towards self-mastery, which is an act of the will. The radical departure entails shedding one's former mindset and a total disconnection from principles that are at variance with the Christian's new state. The mixing of principles of both the old and the new ways amounts to a contradiction and constitutes a serious hindrance to the attainment of self-mastery. The Christian journey towards self-mastery entails constantly listening to the words, "You have heard how it was said," as a constant reminder that old things have passed away. Humans need to realise they have the capacity to overcome their weaknesses and untamed excesses. In fact, we are more than conquerors.

Chapter 10

MORE THAN CONQUERORS

"In all these things we are more than conquerors through him who loved us." (Rom. 8:37)

The journey towards self-mastery demands a strong conviction in each human being's capacity to change for the better. This means that God has endowed each human being with the power to conquer his weaknesses and untamed excesses. God has put that power in each one of us. This power in man is the rational faculty by which he can freely initiate and control his own actions.[1] The power resides in the human intellect. But an added advantage for the Christian is the availability of God's grace, which he supplies in abundance for his children to succeed in whatever they do (2 Cor. 12:9).

Self-mastery requires the realisation of the power of the will. A person's awareness of this ability makes a big difference. It is like an eagle hatched and brought up with chickens. It will not know it can soar into the sky until it is guided to a discovery. Human beings who have become victims of their weaknesses and untamed excesses need to discover this ability of "will" in them, activate it, and put it to maximum use to achieve self-conquest. The Psalmist realised his need for God in the struggle for self-mastery and perfection and prayed thus; "Mount a guard over my mouth, a guard at the door of my lips. Check my impulse to speak evil, to share the

[1] CCC, no. 1731.

foul deeds of evil doers" (141:3-4). The struggle towards self-mastery leads to self-fulfilment because the more one does what is right, the freer and happier one becomes.

There is a need to realise and activate the capacity to change. That capacity lies in the will of each human being. Knowing this power gives the person the self-confidence he needs to begin and pursue the task of self-mastery. The "will" in the human being is the capacity to act; to do good or bad, to obey or not to obey, to love or not to love.[2] Our first parents, Adam and Eve, exercised their wills when they decided to eat the forbidden fruit (Gen 3). The children of men also exercised their wills collectively when they decided to embark on the building of the first skyscraper, i.e., the tower of Babel, to make a name for themselves (Gen. 11:1-9). The prodigal son exercised his will when he decided to demand his share of his estate (Luke 15:12). He exercised the same willpower in his decision to return to his father (vs. 18).

Human freedom comprises the voluntary choice made by the human mind.[3] It is an essential part of human freedom. Its exercise is preceded by a dialogue based on known options to the mind. In other words, the human will exercises its choice from options that the mind has foreknowledge of. This is knowledge of the nature of the action and its rightness or wrongness, its permissibility or otherwise. They will voluntarily decide and choose among the options, good or bad, after the intellect has made its judgement. The power to choose what the person wants to do or not to do resides in the will. St. Thomas Aquinas maintains that God made the human will

---

[2] https://www.biblestudytools.com/dictionary/will/.

[3] CCC, no. 1734.

free. Were it not so, all exhortations, counsels, commands, rewards, and punishments would be meaningless.[4]

The capacity and power of a person's will are expressed in the exhibition of willpower. Willpower is a person's persistence with a given task.[5] It is also called self-will.[6] It is determination sustained by hard work. Christians must realise that they do not embark on the struggle for self-mastery in isolation from God. Christians can always count on Christ, like St. Paul, who realised and acknowledged: "I can do all things through him who strengthens me" (Phil. 4:13). The Christian on the journey to attain self-mastery, therefore, has the enormous power of will that has been bestowed on them by God and the ever-present grace of God to assist in the endeavour. With this, the Christian can confidently say, like St. Paul, "we are more than conquerors" (Rom. 8:37). Knowing that we have the capacity for self-conquest, each of us needs to stay focused and avoid blame.

---

[4] Paul J. Green, *A Tour of the Summa of St. Thomas Aquinas*. Bangalore: Theological, 2007. p. 69.

[5] Robert Lamb, "Power of the Will." https://science.howstuffworks.com/life/inside-the-mind-/human-brain/willpowe3.htm.

[6] Fatima, Mehak. https://bornrealist.com/self-will/.

Chapter 11

THE BLAMING BALM

"The man said, 'The woman whom you gave to me to be with me, she gave me fruits from the tree, and I ate'.... The woman said, 'The serpent tricked me, and I ate.'" (Gen. 3:12)

Some people have blamed their way of life. After making wrong choices, they decide to blame others when the consequences catch up with them. Such people use blaming as a balm to evade responsibility and guilt. After eating the forbidden fruit, Adam blamed Eve, who in turn blamed the serpent (Gen. 3:12-13). Without any attempt to dissuade the people, Aaron agreed to make golden gods for them (Exo. 32:1-6). When Moses confronted him, Aaron blamed it on the people (vv. 22-24). In the battle against the Amalekites, King Saul spared the life of King Agag and took the best of the animals, contrary to the instructions of the Prophet Samuel. When the Prophet confronted King Saul, he blamed it on his men (1 Sam. 15:21). One of the two prostitutes who came to King Solomon for justice had killed her child and blamed it on the other (1 Kings 3:16-28). Adam, Eve, Aaron, Saul, and the prostitute made bad choices but decided to blame others.

It actually feels better to blame others. However, blaming is antithetical to attaining self-mastery. A person who blames never takes responsibility for his weaknesses and untamed excesses. One who blames denies responsibility for his wrong decision and therefore scarcely makes amends. Hence, the Holy Bible exhorts Christians to always take responsibility for their wrong choices. St. James wants blamers to realise that the enticement to sin comes from a person's heart (1:14). St. Paul urges each person to blame no one else for his actions but to take responsibility (Gal. 6:5). Leviticus charges people to take responsibility for their actions instead of blaming (5:5). Taking responsibility for one's actions requires great courage anyway.

Drevitch asserts that some people are better at blaming others for their own problems.[1] They do this to justify their wrong choices. They blame anyone else except themselves for every mishap. The blame game has become so deep-seated in such people that it has become part of their character and flows effortlessly. Most blamers either grew up having their way or they adopted blaming as a manipulative tactic.[2]

Blamers make themselves out to be eternal victims of everything that goes wrong, even of their own bad actions. After they have exhibited aberrant behaviour, the eternal victim in them tells them, "It is not my fault." This is because they believe they are never wrong but always right. They are always the judges in their own cases.[3] Blamers never let go of past hurts or offences or experienc-

---

[1] Gary Drevitch (January 11, 2023), "Why Some People Will Always Blame Others," *Psychology Today.* https://www.psychologytoday.com/us/blog/finding-a-new-home/202212/the-surprising-reason-some-people-always-blame-others

[2] Sherrie Hurd (September 1, 2017), "Blame Game and 6 Types of Toxic People Who Love Playing it," *Learning Mind,* https://learning-mind.com/blame-game-toxic-people.

[3] https://www.quora.com./What-do-you-call-someone-who-blames-others-for-their-own-actions10.06.2019.

es. Hence, they often blame their aberrant behaviours on those who hurt or offended them in the past, particularly during their childhood experiences, for their inability to move forward.[4]

Blaming makes the blamer irresponsible. Ruled by the eternal victim mentality, the blamer never hesitates to act as he wants or say what he wants, since, in the final analysis, someone or something else is always responsible for his actions. Some blame it for defensive purposes. Even though they are guilty, they quickly push the blame so that they are not accused. They blame to evade punishment and make heroes of themselves, seeing others being punished for their faults. The contradiction of the blamer, however, is that he would take the praise for any good actions he performs by chance. Blaming is a manifestation of someone who still finds comfort in their lower self.

The blamer is a stagnant person because he never accepts his wrongdoings, let alone takes steps to make amends. A person who shifts blame lives in his childhood. Blamers never grow. They expend a lot of energy looking for someone to blame rather than scrutinising themselves and learning their lesson to improve. Michael J. Straczynski expresses this idea succinctly when he says that, "People spend too much time finding other people to blame, too much energy finding excuses for not being what they are capable of being, and not enough energy putting themselves on the line, growing out of their past, and getting on with their lives".[5]

---

[4] Hurd, "Blame Game".

[5] J. Michael Straczynski, Brainy Quote, https://brainyquote.com/quotes/j_michael_straczynski_125688

The truth remains that anyone who reflects on himself whenever he is at fault is the better for it. These are those who are constantly in touch and in dialogue with their inner selves. Blamers live a false life. They never get in touch with their real selves. They live a divided life; they are never down to earth, scarcely in touch with reality, never truthful to themselves. Consequently, they hardly experience true conversion. They blame to excuse themselves of their weaknesses and untamed excesses. In journeying towards self-mastery, one must avoid a life of blaming. According to Jeremy Binns, "The day you stop blaming others is the day you begin to discover who you truly are".[6]

Blamers need help. They need to be tolerated and helped to overcome their false life and stagnation. It is important to state here that tolerance does not suggest approval. It does not suggest that innocent people should accept blame from blamers or cover them up. It is important, rather, to help them in charity, to realise the need to own up to their actions and words. They need to be made to realise the harm in being blamers and the need to be guided by wisdom in their choices.[7] To conquer oneself and attain self-mastery, therefore, a person has to stop blaming and take full responsibility for the outcomes of his actions.

Blamers need to learn to evaluate whatever they want to do or say in their rational faculties before letting them out. They also need to realise that they have the freedom to carry out their actions or not and to take full responsibility afterward, for it is in taking responsibility that we overcome our failures. John C. Maxwell puts

---

[6] Ibid.

[7] Ibid.

this succinctly: "People who blame others for their failures never overcome them. They move from problem to problem. To reach your potential, you must continually improve yourself, and you can't do that if you don't take responsibility for your actions and learn from them".[8] Proverbs 28:13 teaches that the secret of a progressive life is to deal with one's failure. It is about acknowledging one's faults, repenting of them, and learning from them. King David is quite exemplary on this. He confessed as soon as he realised he had done wrong (cf. 2 Sam. 12:13; Psalm 51:3-40).

There is another side to the blame. Some blame themselves for everything that ever goes wrong, even when they absolutely had nothing to do with what went wrong.[9] Such people believe, most or all the time, that they are the cause of everything that goes wrong. They assume culpability for what they are not culpable for. Moral theology refers to such people as having scrupulous consciences.[10] It is an anomaly that such people need help to overcome. They need help understanding what constitutes a wrong action and taking blame only for actions for which they are culpable and responsible. It is necessary to live a life of virtue, which is the vehicle for attaining self-mastery.

---

[8] Ibid.

[9] https://www.google.com/amp/s/www.psychologytoday.com/intl/blog/fulfiillment-any-age/201509 10.06.2019.

[10] Thomas Pazhayampallil, Pastoral Guide vol. I. Bangalore, Kristy Jyoti, 2004. P. 232.

Chapter 12

THE VICTIM MENTALITY

"We are afflicted in every way, but not crushed; perplexed, but not driven to despair; persecuted, but not forsaken; struck down, but not destroyed."
(2 *Cor.* 4:88-9)

The struggle towards self-mastery is that of faith. It is a struggle towards becoming who God created us and desires us to be - perfect as himself (Matt. 5:48). However, one major drawback in this struggle is the victim mentality. This mentality refers to a frame of mind in which a person puts themselves in the position of being a casualty in almost everything that goes wrong and affects them. The mindset makes the person feel as though he is the one being targeted whenever something bad happens, resulting in his suffering. The person considers himself to be the one always being opposed, maltreated, or subjected to hardship. For any bad thing that happens, he never considers himself to be the cause but someone else. Nothing is ever the person's fault.[1] Even when he is the oppressor, he believes he is the one being oppressed. A person with this mentality never takes responsibility but always blames others for whatever goes wrong that affects them. The victim mentality leads a person to live in self-pity and always feel sorry for themselves, even for the bad things they caused.

---

[1] https://folcc.org/the-biblical-way-to-overcome-victim-mentality-and-be-a-victor/.

Whenever they have a bad experience, people with a victim mentality do not think they caused it. They believe that something happened to them, or that someone or something did it. According to Akos Balogh, people with the victim mentality see their entire lives through the lens that things constantly happen to them. They see most things in life as negative, beyond their control, and as things they deserve sympathy for. Balogh points out that at its heart, a victim mentality is a way of avoiding responsibility for one's life. Simply put, any bad thing that happens in his life is not his fault but the fault of others. The other people are the ones who are bad, wrong, or dumb, while he is good, right, and brilliant. It is only other people who do bad or stupid things, and he suffers as a result.[2]

There are a few indicators that help identify people with the victim mentality. Firstly, they are mostly extremely self-centered. They reduce everything in life to themselves. They will rarely ever ask you anything about yourself. You can sit with them and talk for a couple of hours, and it will never occur to them to ask you anything.

Secondly, they complain. Their victim mentality leads them to complain about everything that happens to them, since nothing is ever their fault. Thirdly, the pattern of their thinking causes them to hold on to every injustice, every hurt, every pain, and they refuse to let go. They keep them and tell the stories passionately to but-

---

[2] Akos Balogh, https://au-thegospelcoalition-org.cdn.ampproject.org/v/s/au.

tress and convince anyone who listens to them that they are victims.[3]

No one is completely free from this victim mentality. Almost every person has at one time or another given in to the victim mentality. However, upon realising this, many struggle to overcome it because of their lack of maturity. Unfortunately, some others decide to make it part of their life and nature. This mentality eventually becomes one of the defining characteristics of such people.

Perhaps some people enjoy playing the victim because it has subtle benefits. They may get attention and validation. They enjoy some attention from others who may extend a willing hand of help out of pity. However, this attention does not last because the people eventually get tired. Also, those who play the victim often don't dare take risks. They would not want to take the risk lest they fail. They are comfortable with just staying and having others do things for them.[4] People with the victim mentality feel inferior and defeated. They see themselves as helpless victims of oppression by any other person.

Certain circumstances and life experiences can lead a person to adopt a victim mentality. For instance, a woman who loses her beloved husband or a child who loses a parent, or both parents, tends to develop a victim mentality. A child brought up by either a parent or parents who have a victim mentality may develop the same. A child who is abused or maltreated to the point of injuring their self-worth and esteem could develop a victim mentality.

---

[3] https://folcc.org/the-biblical-way-to-overcome-victim-mentality-and-be-a-victor/.

[4] Ibid.

While talking about the victim mentality, it is worth stating that there are people who have actually been victimised in the real sense of it. These are innocent people who have suffered at the hands of wicked people. In the Scriptures, God himself condemns the oppression of the innocent. The Book of Zechariah speaks strongly against the oppression of the weak (7:10). Jesus himself suffered human wickedness (cf. Isa. 53:6-7; Luke 23:15-16; Acts 3:14-15). However, people should be cautious about adopting a victim mentality simply because they have been victimised.

When the Israelites, at the bank of the Red Sea, saw Pharaoh's army, a victim mentality came upon them overwhelmingly. The same people who had prayed all the years for liberation from Egypt to return to the promised land where they could worship their God, began blaming Moses (Exo. 14:10-11). Moses turned to God, and God responded that there was no need for panic (vv. 15-16). Despite all the victimisation, Jesus never took on the victim mentality. He rather suffered lovingly and bled for those who victimised him (1 Peter 2:21-24) and prayed for their forgiveness (Luke 23:34). When the apostles were persecuted, they did not give in to the victim mentality but instead, rejoiced that they were privileged to suffer for Christ and went on teaching every day in the Temple and at home (Acts 5:41-42). St. Paul did not give in to the victim mentality, either. He was proud to suffer hardship for the sake of the Gospel of Christ (2 Cor. 12:10).

The victim mentality is highly inimical to the journey towards self-mastery. It constitutes a grave disservice to a person's life in general, stunts personal growth, and is an enemy of the journey towards self-mastery. Balogh points some of them out. First, the victim mentality distorts a person's view of reality by making them see things through a negative lens. The person magnifies the bad things that happen to him and attributes them exclusively to other people and to forces outside himself.[5]

Second, those with the victim mentality exaggerate harm done to them and downplay their faults or even play them away completely. The victim in them reasons that, after all, their faults are nothing compared to what others have done to them. The victim mentality constructs a false narrative that explains one's situation, placing blame exclusively on other people or circumstances.[6] A natural consequence is that, when one is blind to one's own faults, one will also be blind to one's need for change and growth.

Third, the victim mentality disempowers people by removing nearly all their initiative to improve their situation. They lose the ability to influence their circumstances and improve their lives positively. In other words, they are held hostage to their circumstances and cannot grow.[7]

Fourth, the victim mentality sucks joy out of people's lives because it hinders them from seeing God's blessings and being thankful for them. This mentality is dangerous because it not only distorts and magnifies people's difficulties but also blurs their view of their blessings. Those who see only their difficulties and get frus-

---

[5] Akos Balogh, https://au-thegospelcoalition-org.cdn.ampproject.org/v/s/au.

[6] Ibid.

[7] Ibid.

trated by them lack the capacity to notice their blessings.[8] Hence, joy eludes them.

Fifth, the victim mentality damages relationships. Since they are convinced that others are responsible for the bad things that happen to them, their relationship with those people is damaged. A person with the victim mentality will naturally hold bitterness and anger towards their perceived aggressor and avoid any relationship with them.[9]

Sixth, the victim mentality could lead a person to despair. The mentality involves a feeling of helplessness in the hands of an oppressor or the circumstances. This disposition can eat deeper into a person's psyche, leading to despair. When this happens, the individual loses the hope of developing the capacity to take responsibility for his actions.

Balogh counsels that since the foremost victim of human history [Jesus Christ] never adopted the victim mentality, it is not a biblical response to unjust suffering. Therefore, it has no place in the journey towards self-mastery since it involves the determination to conquer one's weaknesses and untamed excesses. This is a journey of faith that is by no means easy to undertake. Like any other good thing in life, the journey towards self-mastery is at a cost. One will encounter challenges. Therefore, instead of taking on the victim mentality, one needs to pay heed to St. James' admonition to consider the challenges as trials which, when faced, produce steadfastness whose effect is the attainment of perfection and completion: *"Count it all joy, my brethren, when you meet various trials, for you*

---

[8] Ibid.

[9] Ibid.

know that the testing of your faith produces steadfastness. And let steadfastness have its full effect, that you may be perfect and complete, lacking in nothing" (James 1:2-4). This perfection and completion are the goal of self-mastery. St Paul insists that no number of challenging experiences can make a person give up by developing a victim mentality. He states: *"We are afflicted in every way, but not crushed; perplexed, but not driven to despair; persecuted, but not forsaken; struck down, but not destroyed"* (2 *Cor.* 4:8-9)

Chapter 13

SELF-ACCOUNTABILITY

"For I know my transgressions, and my sin is ever before me." (Psalm 51:3)

The struggle to attain self-mastery requires self-accountability. This is a journey of self-discipline that demands the individual evaluate progress and failures at certain points in the struggle. It happens through meditations and reflections. In doing this, the individual holds himself accountable. No meaningful progress can be made in this struggle if one cannot hold oneself accountable.

Self-accountability is understood variously. Here, it refers to a person's ability to hold himself liable for his actions, decisions, in-actions, and indecisions, as the case may be. It presupposes that the person has a goal to attain and has resolved and set standards to live by. The person, therefore, takes full responsibility for progress or failure made in the endeavour to achieve his goal. It is a situation in which one holds oneself answerable for one's decisions and conduct.

Self-accountability is a conscientious art that involves self-examination and interrogation. Each conscientious person has an internal court, a faculty for self-scrutiny within him called conscience, which is treated in chapter thirty-two. This internal court holds one accountable. It scrutinises one's decisions and actions against set goals and internalised values from culture, religion, education, and, above all, the backdrop of natural justice. In self-accountability, a person can call themselves out for their actions, inactions, and missteps. Self-accountability takes place in one's conscience, a natural faculty God has endowed each human being with. It is, however, necessary that as one grows, one makes an effort to form one's conscience with the Word of God, the teachings of the Church, and other norms of right reason. This is further treated in chapter thirty-two.

An accountable person does not excuse or mollify oneself. Instead, the person holds themself accountable and may blame or praise himself or herself as necessary. The person then takes clear and decisive stands on issues as the need arises. By Self-accountability, one demands a purposeful commitment from oneself.[1]

There is a common human tendency to sit on a self-acclaimed forthrightness to criticise other people. However, the same person feels deeply uneasy when criticised. A sense of self-accountability flows from the awareness of the reality of our human nature: no one is without faults, and each person has a binding responsibility to hold themselves accountable.[2]

The ability for self-accountability requires courage. It is necessary to enable the person to accuse himself, demand an explanation for his decisions and behaviour, and pass a verdict on them. Even with the right actions, the person can assess and explore ways to improve. Courage helps the individual to beam the searchlight on areas where one is not measuring up and face them squarely instead of engaging in unnecessary rationalisation.

---

[1] https//www.partnersinlesdership.com. 27.08.2021.

[2] https://www.gr8tness.com. 27.08.2021.

King David is one Biblical figure who held himself accountable. Upon realising that he had sinned against the Lord, he confessed; *"I have sinned against the Lord"* (2 Sam. 12:13). He was moved to contrition which he expressed in Psalm 50/51: *"For I know my transgressions, and my sin is ever before me"* (v. 3).

Self-accountability paves the way for self-reproach. By it, a person forestalls future occurrences and gains the courage to make resolutions that are not mere cosmetic propositions but concrete, definite, and tangible resolves that serve as principles to guide one's life.

In self-accountability, one does not shy away or ignore one's shortcomings. Rather, one faces and deals with them. Where a person has tried, they applaud and may decide to reward themselves. Conversely, when the person has failed or performed below their set targets, they reprimand themselves. The person could even impose certain deprivations and restrictions on himself to sanction and punish himself. It is important to point out, however, that deprivations and restrictions to be imposed should neither be harsh nor injurious to the person.

Notably, a person who lives a life of self-accountability is sometimes perceived by others who pay no attention to such a life as being hard on himself. They may embark on persuasions on the person to develop sympathy for himself so that he can lower his bars. When this happens, growth gets stunted, and the journey towards self-mastery is frustrated.

Chapter 14

THE VIRTUE VEHICLE

"For this very reason, make every effort to supplement your faith with virtue."
(2 Peter 1:5)

Socrates is said to have been the first to express the belief that human effort is necessary to attain happiness. To achieve this, he recommended that one must gain rational control over one's desires and harmonise the different parts of one's soul. He believed that doing so would produce a divine-like state of inner tranquillity that the external world could not affect.[1] The happiness Socrates refers to is not a feeling of elation, excitement, or pleasure that comes from some gratification,[2] which is momentary and transient. The happiness Socrates refers to is a state of the mind; an internal state of peace and tranquillity. This kind of happiness is a natural consequence of attaining self-mastery.

Following Socrates, Aristotle maintained that a person who has attained a good degree of self-mastery craves only for the things he ought, as he ought, and when he ought.[3] This means that the person desires only the right things and does them at the right time, in the right manner, and under the right circumstances. Such a person does only what ought to be done in the right manner and at the

---

[1] https://www.pursuit-of-happiness.org.

[2] The New International Webster's Comprehensive Dictionary of the English Language. Florida: Typhoon, 2004.

[3] https://www.skillsyouneed.com.

right moment. Aristotle advocates that this kind of acting should be made a habit by which virtue is cultivated. Virtue here refers to the habitual carrying out of a good action that becomes part of a person's character. Aristotle identifies this as the secret of true happiness. Plato toed the same line by holding that happiness and well-being are the aims of moral thought and conduct. He advocates a life of virtue, along with the skills and dispositions needed to attain it.[4]

Christian theology understands virtue in both wider and narrower senses. In the wider sense, it is "Any perfectly developed capacity of man's spiritual soul or the development itself".[5] In its narrow sense, "Virtue is the power (ability, skill, facility) to realise moral good, and especially to do it joyfully and perseveringly even against inner and outer obstacles and at the cost of sacrifice".[6] The Catechism of the Catholic Church explains that a virtue is a habitual and firm disposition to do good.[7] It enables a person not only to perform good deeds but also to give their best. The person can pursue good and choose it always in concrete situations. The goal of living a virtuous life, therefore, is to become like God.[8] This is the essence of attaining self-mastery.

---

[4] https://www.iep.utm.edu/aris-eth.

[5] Karl Rahner, "Virtue" in *Encyclopedia of Theology: A Concise Sacramentum Mundi.* Edited by Karl Rahner. Mumbai: St. Paul, 2004.

[6] Ibid.

[7] CCC, no. 1833.

[8] CCC, no 1803.

Trese talks of virtue as a habit or a permanent disposition that inclines a person to do good and avoid evil.[9] St. Thomas Aquinas believed that people who attained any level of self-mastery were those who were persistent in doing what is right: "They were able to do the right things to keep themselves healthy and happy."[10] The best way to live a happy life, according to Aquinas, is to live a life of virtue, which he refers to as the disposition to do good at all times to all people. Aquinas believes that a happy state of life is attainable by a life of virtue. Hence, the four cardinal virtues are instrumental, namely, prudence, temperance, courage, and justice.[11] The first three virtues make us good people, while justice guides our relationship with others and makes us good citizens.

The virtue of "Prudence disposes the [our] practical reason to discern, in every circumstance, our true good and to choose the right means for achieving it".[12] It helps us make good judgements about how we should behave. Aquinas refers to it as "wisdom concerning human affairs" or "right reason with regards to action". Prudence makes us exercise command over our actions. Temperance is the virtue that "Moderates the attraction of the pleasures of the senses and provides balance in the use of created goods".[13] It is the disposition by which we restrain our desires for physical gratification. Temperance moderates our attraction to bodily pleasure

---

[9] Leo J. Trese, *The Faith Explained.* Lagos: Criterion, 2007. P. 131.

[10] https://www.skillsyouneed.com.

[11] https://www.iep.utm.edu/aris-eth.

[12] CCC, no. 1835.

[13] CCC, no. 1838.

and provides a balance in our use of created things.[14] Courage restrains our fears so that we might endure harrowing experiences. It is also called fortitude. It is the virtue that "Ensures firmness in difficulties and constancy in the pursuit of the good".[15] The virtue enables us to conquer fear and makes us firm in times of difficulty, and gives us constancy in the pursuit of good.[16] The virtue of justice governs our relationship with God and others. This virtue "Consists in the firm and constant will to give God and neighbour their due".[17] It is the willingness to extend to God and our neighbor what they deserve.[18]

The Christian on the journey towards self-mastery necessarily needs to live a life of virtue. They have to integrate the four cardinal virtues into their lives. The more he integrates them, the more he grows in self-mastery. In short, the life of virtue is indispensable in the struggle to attain self-mastery. Virtue is actually a vehicle for the journey towards self-mastery. The next chapter explains that everything we know of, including virtue, is meant to be put into practice.

---

[14] CCC, no. 1809.

[15] CCC, no. 1837.

[16] CCC, no. 1808.

[17] CCC, no. 1836.

[18] https://www.iep.utm.edu/aris-eth.

Chapter 15

LIVE WHAT YOU KNOW

"The scribes and the Pharisees sit on Moses' seat; so practice and observe whatever they tell you, but not what they do; for they preach but do not practice."
(Matt. 23:2-3)

One of the points of Jesus' discomfort with the scribes and Pharisees was that they were religious intellectual giants but moral dwarfs. Even though they had extensive knowledge of the law and religious traditions and could offer accurate interpretations, they could not translate that knowledge into concrete actions. Hence, he cautioned his followers, "The scribes and the Pharisees sit on Moses' seat; so practice and observe whatever they tell you, but not what they do; for they preach but do not practice" (Matt. 23:2-3).

Knowledge about Christ is a major resource factor in the struggle towards attaining self-mastery. Authentic Christian human development is not measured merely by a person's intellectual property but by the degree to which the knowledge acquired has been implemented, resulting in self-mastery. Knowledge of Christ is good, but it is not an end in itself. Self-mastery is an object of acquiring knowledge. Knowledge of Christ is acquired in order to effect a change of behaviour. Such knowledge is of no benefit to a Christian who lacks the commensurate moral altitude. Expectedly, therefore, the more knowledgeable a person is, the more refined and the higher his moral pedigree should be. It is a noble thing for a Christian to live out what he knows. The Christian must use his knowledge of God as an instrument for the attainment of self-mastery.

It will therefore amount to a sad reality to find a religious intellectual who has conquered books and libraries but has not conquered himself. The Russian dramatist Anton Chekhov is quoted to have said that, "Knowledge is of no value unless you put it into practice".[1] It will amount to a contradiction if a person attains religious intellectual mastery without attaining self-mastery. Greeting pilgrims on May 7, 2014, Pope Francis warns about the danger of the Christian who sees religious knowledge as only a matter of the mind. The Pope told the pilgrims that Christians must translate their knowledge into concrete action with openness to the Holy Spirit.[2] Knowledge of Christ should be the antidote to our weaknesses and untamed excesses, which manifest in our aberrant actions. This is the goal of Christian education. Pope Paul VI stated that Catholic education aims to form the human person for maturity.[3] A well-formed Christian education program is designed to develop a person's intellectual capacities, enhancing their ability to judge well and make the right decisions.[4] This is indeed what self-mastery is about.

Through the prophet Hosea, God laments thus: "My people are destroyed for lack of knowledge" (4:6). A person who acquires knowledge but is unable to put it into practice, neglecting its de-

---

[1] https://www.brainyquote.com/quotes/anton_chekhov_119058.

[2] https://www.catholicnewsagency.com./news/pope-warns-against-close-mindedness-of-intellectual-aristocracy.

[3] *Gravissimum Educationis*, no. 1.

[4] *Gravissimum Educationis*, no. 5.

mands, suffers the same fate. Again, restating the accusation of Christ to the Pharisees and the Scribes; "This people honours me only with their lips, but their hearts are far away from me" (Matt. 15:8). It is a scandal to accumulate knowledge about Christ without translating it into practice. They fit into our Lord's analogy of the servant who knows what the master wants but has not put it into practice (Luke 12:47).

There is therefore a need to work for and pray for the gift of wisdom, which is the thread that knits knowledge, objectivity, and goodwill, resulting in good choices. When knowledge lacks the wisdom to guard and guide it, its application can be manipulated by self-interest, resulting in mere exhibitions of smartness and shrewdness that do no good to anyone. Wisdom plays a vital role in coordinating knowledge and putting it into practice. When a person has attained self-mastery also, the person's life is characterised by the same wisdom. In the next chapter, we will see that one way we know God's mind is through hearing. The hearer must make efforts to put what he hears into practice.

Chapter 16

HEARERS AND DOERS

"But be doers of the word, and not merely hearers who deceive themselves." (James 1:22)

In Christendom today, more people are claiming to hear God speak to them directly. Yet, there is almost nothing of godly conduct seen in their lives. Such people emphasised spiritual powers without a corresponding emphasis on self-conquest. They claim to have one spiritual power or another, while their weaknesses and untamed excesses manifest as aberrant behaviour on a rampage. Consequently, it is common to find a person who considers himself a "powerful man of God," claiming to command evil spiritual powers out of people. At the same time, the excesses in him remain untamed. We see claims that they have conquered certain forces and control large followings without having conquered themselves. They cheaply attribute any manifestation of their weaknesses and untamed excesses to the devil.

Some of those claiming spiritual powers parading themselves as "Men of God" have been reported to be involved in despicable acts. For instance, the Punch Newspaper of 28th April, 2018, reported that a "man of God" was arrested for kidnapping.[1] Punch Newspaper, 5th May, 2017, reported the arrest of "a man of God" in possession of a human head.[2] The Guardian Newspaper of 26th

---

[1] https://punching.com.

[2] https://punching.com.

June, 2018, reported the confession of a pastor who killed for ritual purposes.[3] Several concerns have also been expressed about extortions of money in Churches by some avaricious pastors.[4] There are also incidents of the involvement of men of God in sex scandals.[5] These examples demonstrate how people claim possession of spiritual powers without self-mastery.

This situation is not peculiar only to men of God. Some Church members are also involved. In some of the cases cited above, church members are accomplices, making themselves willing tools in the hands of such "men of God". Also, there is the challenge of a lack of self-mastery. Over time, when criminals are arrested, some of them are found to be Christians. Today, there are rampant cases of lustful behaviours, divorce, stealing, vengeful anger, and exploitation in businesses, etc. These are all expressions of unconquered weaknesses and untamed excesses.

Perhaps all of these are not happening by accident, because we are running into a situation where most preachers either do not preach at all on the need to live virtuous lives, or do not preach about it enough. The attention of many preachers has shifted to miracles, tongues, signs, and wonders. Other preachers try their best to teach their people how to live a life of virtue. However, it does not reflect in the lives of some of the members.

People attend masses, retreats, crusades, and vigils where they pray, sing, dance, clap and make donations which are sometimes fat. Good as these practices are, there is almost no corresponding

---

[3] https://t.guardian.ng.

[4] https://www.ghanaweb.com.

[5] https://www.christianweek.org.

manifestation in terms of their mastery over themselves. Instead, much is seen of a raw display of weaknesses, excesses, and aberrant tendencies. Many have become very opinionated and hold tenaciously to their personal desires and wishes above gospel values. This is a problem of double allegiance between the idolised self and God. In this case, the person makes himself his own master and decides to place his loyalty in himself rather than in God. Jesus warns, "No one can serve two masters" (Matt. 6:24).

Some Christians have an exaggerated understanding of grace to the point of believing that nothing in their conduct, good or bad, matters for their salvation. The Catechism of the Catholic Church echoes St. Augustine's words: "God created us without us; but he did not will to save us without us."[6] Jesus states unambiguously, "Not everyone who says to me 'Lord, Lord', shall enter the Kingdom of heaven, but he who does the will of my Father who is in heaven" (Mt 7:21). Does this negate the place of grace in Christian Life? No. Grace basically assists the Christian in finding the strength and perseverance to carry out good works. Grace makes it easier for the Christian to do good.

No doubt, the Christian is saved and made pure gratuitously by God. This is pure grace. However, the sustenance of this purity requires an individual struggle. This is where the individual effort in doing good comes in. It is an effort to live a virtuous life by which the person not only performs good acts but gives the best of himself.[7] This act of doing good entails conquering and subduing

---

[6] CCC, no. 1847.

[7] CCC, no. 1803.

our weaknesses and untamed excesses, which manifest as aberrant behaviours, thereby leading to self-mastery. St. Paul encourages the Philippians; "Whatever is true, whatever is honourable, whatever is just, whatever is pure, whatever is lovely, whatever is gracious if there is anything excellent, if there is anything worthy of praise, think about these things. What you have learned and received and heard and seen in me, do; and the God of peace will be with you" (Phil 4:8-9). To attain self-mastery, the Christian must be a hearer and a doer: St. James exhorts: "But be doers of the Word, and not hearers only, deceiving yourselves" (1:22).

Chapter 17

TAMING THE TONGUE

"Honour and dishonour come from speaking, and the tongue of mortals may be their downfall." (Sirach 5:13)

The tongue is an organ in the mouth used for tasting and speaking. "Tongue" could mean a particular way of speaking or writing.[1] What this means is that the tongue is a metaphor for a person's utterances, either spoken or written. It can be used constructively or destructively. The tongue can bring a person both good and bad. With the tongue, one can make a multitude of friends or a multitude of enemies. A person can gain acceptance or rejection by his tongue, honour or dishonour, respect or disrespect, praise, or denunciation. The tongue can lift a person and bring a person down, exalt a person, or humiliate a person.

It has the power to build or destroy (Prov. 10:11). We can praise God with the tongue, and we can blaspheme against God with it. The tongue can send a person forward and hold a person back. It can say helpful words and harmful words. The tongue can transform and deform lives. The tongue can make a person acceptable or detestable. It can speak truth, and it can speak falsehood. The tongue can initiate both peace and war. The tongue can make one attain heaven, and it can make one go to hell. Hence, one

[1] *Macmillan English Dictionary for Advanced Learners. Second Edition.* Oxford: Macmillan, 2007.

can talk of a sharp tongue to refer to an unkind way of speaking as well as a silver tongue to mean the ability to talk well.[2]

Self-mastery requires a person to watch their tongue. It is necessary to tame the tongue and bring it under control. The tongue that speaks anything, anyhow, at any time, to anyone, is untamed. A tamed tongue utters no destructive but constructive words. It says the right things only to the right person, only at the right time, and only at the right occasion. A tamed tongue speaks only when it needs to. A tamed tongue speaks only when it should speak and shuts up when it should. It does not speak unnecessarily. A tamed tongue is a moderated tongue. And, of course, the tongue actually merely reflects what a person has in the heart for the mouth speaks out of the abundance of the heart (Matt. 12:34; Prov. 4:23); for a tree is known by its fruits (Matt. 12: 33).

A refined man or woman is a person who has attained appreciable degrees of self-mastery and is known by two indicators - physical appearance and a modest tongue. A tamed tongue does not speak too much. It is not loose with words and is not unnecessarily verbose. A person with a tamed tongue is not quick and imposing with his opinions. A tamed tongue does not delight in putting others down. It does not trade in sarcasm.[3] The tongue that is tamed is diligent and slow to speak (James 1:19). And being gentlemanly is a sign of religiosity. That is why St. James further teaches that the real test of one who claims to be religious is in the disci-

---

[2] *Macmillan English Dictionary for Advanced Learners. Second Edition.* Oxford: Macmillan, 2007.

[3] http://www.keepbelieving.com/sermon/how-to-tame-the-terrible-tongue/.

pline of his tongue; "If any think they are religious, and do not bridle their tongues but deceive their hearts, their religion is worthless" (James 1:26). A refined man or woman knows when to speak (Sirach 20:6). The wise remain silent and speak only at the right moment (vs. 7).

The tongue is like fire. Fire warms a cold place; it produces light that could be used for cooking. However, a tiny spark of fire can burn down a vast forest that may take several years to regrow. In the same way, a tamed tongue can bring warmth and build bridges in a community. But an untamed tongue is deadly and can burn communities down, just as a forest fire does. It destroys a person's reputation and deters others from associating with the individual. An untamed tongue poisons relationships and breeds disunity. The Book of Sirach warns: "Do not be called double-tongued and do not lay traps with your tongue" (5:14).

Taming the tongue means to bring one's utterances under control. A person who can bring his tongue under control can avoid many troubles. The wise author of the book of Proverbs says, "He who guards his mouth and his tongue keeps himself from trouble" (21:23). St. James believes that those who bring their tongues under control will be perfect and can have control over themselves, for the tongue is a small member of the body but with great exploits (3:2-5). The tongue is so powerful that he expresses concern that no one on his own can tame it without God's help. He refers to an untamed tongue as "a restless evil, full of deadly poison" (3:8). There is emphasis on taming the tongue because it recognises the power of life and death in it (Prov. 18:21). It teaches that the words of the reckless pierce like swords. In contrast, the tongue of the wise brings healing (12:18). The Psalmist prays to God to set a guard on his mouth and keep watch over the door of his lips (141:3).

There are certain situations under which a tamed tongue does not speak. The first is when a person is very angry. In this situation, one may say very unruly and unprintable things opposed to right reason and common sense, and one becomes enveloped in regrets after the anger is gone. According to Proverbs, it is only a fool who gives full vent to his anger. The wise man holds his anger back (29:11). The second situation is extreme excitement. In this condition, many have made promises they regretted after the excitement wore off. Herod committed such a blunder (Mark 6:21-29).

The tongue needs to be tamed because whatever comes out of it cannot be taken back. Once the tongue has spoken words, they cannot be taken back; if they are good, they remain in the receiver's memory. If they are bad, they also remain. It is like the proverbial spilling of the beans. What an untamed tongue releases is poison that cannot be taken back. The most that can be done afterward is damage control. This situation can be compared to when poison has found its way into the human body. Doctors can only try to mitigate the maximum harm it could cause to the body. Therefore, it is good and necessary to tame the tongue so that its utterances can be modest and constructive. Taming the tongue is necessary in the effort towards attaining self-mastery. Also, a tamed tongue is a sign of one who has attained self-mastery. A common error that could be made by many is to mistake an untamed tongue for being courageous.

Chapter 18

PRUNING OUTCOME

"Every branch that bears no fruit he [the Father] prunes to make it bear more fruit." (John 15:2)

This is a true-life story. I grew up to find a sweet, fruit-bearing mango tree in our family compound. At the time of writing this book, my father told me that it had been there for more than sixty years and was still bearing fruit. Occasionally, our dad brought someone to prune the tree. The first time I saw it done, I was angry that the cutting would reduce the quantity of fruit the tree would produce from then on. I decided to ask my dad why he was bringing people to cut down the tree's branches. He explained to me that the tree was trimmed either when it became infected or when its branches grew old. It was pruned to allow it to regenerate by sprouting new branches, thereby enabling it to bear more, healthier, and sweeter fruits.

Pruning is familiar to horticulturalists. They do trim their plants or trees occasionally to enable new growth and optimal productivity. Pruning means to remove parts of a tree or plant to make it grow better.[1] It means trimming or cutting superfluous branches or parts to improve growth.[2] It also means to get rid of

---

[1] *Macmillan English Dictionary for Advance Learners.* Oxford: Macmillan, 2007.

[2] *The New Webster's Comprehensive Dictionary.* Naples: Trident, 2004.

something you do not need or want, especially to reduce its size or cut it off.[3] In the context of the endeavour to attain self-mastery, it means to trim or cut down our weaknesses and untamed excesses. These constitute a heavy burden on the Christian, weighing him down and thereby preventing him from living a virtuous life. There is therefore the need to trim them down to give way for new and godly characters to sprout.

Jesus used the gardening metaphor to describe the importance of spiritual pruning. The one who prunes is God himself. He prunes every branch that bears fruit so that it can begin to bear fruit again. The branches that bear fruit, he prunes so that they can bear more fruit (John 15:2). Jesus is the vine. God is the vine dresser. Jesus' disciples are the branches. In this analogy, the vine is constant, consistently good, and productive. Therefore, the activity is directed towards the branches, i.e., the disciples. It is the branch that could depreciate in bearing fruit and needs to be pruned to bear fruit. God also prunes even the fruitful branches occasionally so that they can be even more fruitful.[4]

Pruning is an integral part of and a necessary condition for moral and spiritual fruitfulness. It is a personal, continuous endeavour, and it is painful. We cannot say that the vine was pruned over two thousand years ago and therefore needs no pruning today. Jesus does not desire that his disciples' lives be stunted. Hence, as long as a disciple lives and is connected to him, the disciple needs pruning. A disciple who is not pruned eventually experiences

---

[3] *Macmillan English Dictionary for Advance Learners.* Oxford: Macmillan, 2007.

[4] *The International Bible Commentary.* Bangalore: Theological, 2007.

wear and tear and exhaustion and thus begins to depreciate in good works.

The Word of God is the axe for the pruning. All that is required of the disciple is to surrender to the loving care of God, take his words to heart, and put them into practice. Then, the effect of the Word will manifest in the pruning of the disciple.[5] God's Word is meant to prune the disciple, thereby causing new, refined, productive characters to sprout, just as the rain that never returns without watering the earth brings new sprouts, seeds to the sower, and food for the eater (Isa. 55:10).

The analogy and theology of pruning are quite relevant in the struggle to attain self-mastery. It can be stepped down to refer to the act of pruning our weaknesses and untamed excesses. The Christian must constantly willingly allow himself to be pruned by God's axe – the Word of God. He must make every effort to internalise the contents of the Word of God he listens to every day of his life. The disciple of Christ must always take the Word of God and sound exhortations given during the homily at Mass to heart and make a concerted effort to implement its content. He must always find time to meditate on the word of God, which he has listened to, and make a serious effort to apply it with concerted deliberateness. This is how he can, day by day, eliminate his weaknesses and untamed excesses and eventually conquer them. This means that each time God's Word is proclaimed, the disciple is expected to mirror and appropriate it for himself, not for another person.

---

[5] *The International Bible Commentary.* Bangalore: Theological, 2007.

We cannot ignore the fact that every tree bleeds as it is being pruned. This shows that pruning is painful. In the same way, the disciple needs to know that the process of pruning one's weaknesses and untamed excesses can also be very painful. It is especially so for those behaviours that have taken deep roots in our lives and have become like our second nature. The disciple must be courageous to face it. This is where the disciple needs personal discipline and strong willpower. Pruning is painful, but the benefits are good; it is a means of cleansing, reshaping, and purification.[6] The disciple needs to treat the Word of God and every sound homily as directives, not as optional advice subject to debate.

Preachers, therefore, have a challenge to prepare their homilies in such a way that they convey sound faith and morals in accordance with the mind of God. Adequately prepared sound homilies are effective and yield the desired purposes of pruning, leading to the attainment of self-mastery. Preachers need to take care not to package homilies as mere entertainment materials. They are never to use the pulpit for show-off but to bear in mind that the words from their mouths are God's and they are the axe for pruning God's disciples so that those "under-fruiting" can begin to produce optimally and those that are fruiting can produce even more fruits. It should never be heard that either on account of the preacher or the hearer, God's Word returns to God without accomplishing its purpose.

---

[6] https://www.arynthelibrary.com/pruning -in-the-bible. 17.06.2019.

Chapter 19

SUBSTITUTION STRATEGY

"You were taught to put away your former way of life, your old self, corrupt and deluded by its lusts, and to be renewed in the spirit of your minds and to clothe yourselves with the new self, created according to the likeness of God in true righteousness." (Eph. 4:22-24)

Substitution is the act of replacing something or someone with another.[1] Simply put, it means removing something and putting something else in its place. This can also be referred to as displacement and replacement. The struggle towards attaining self-mastery requires the constant disposition and readiness to substitute. The disciple must always be ready to displace his negative character traits stemming from his weaknesses and untamed excesses, and replace them with new ones in accordance with the gospel values. This is how a life of virtue is built. It involves constant displacement and replacement. The individual displaces whatever is antithetical to attaining self-mastery with values of virtue. This cannot be taken for granted in the struggle towards self-mastery.

The journey towards attaining self-mastery is essentially a struggle to conquer one's weaknesses and untamed excesses. The rule of substitutions is necessary in this struggle. For any negative attitude the person decides to throw out of his life, a vacuum is cre-

[1] *Macmillan English Dictionary for Advance Learners.* Oxford: Macmillan, 2007.

ated which he must fill with a positive attitude. If the vacuum is not filled, the specific negative thing the person threw away will find its way back, or the person himself may return to it. This is in accordance with the Aristotelian fundamental natural principle that nature abhors a vacuum.[2]

Jesus underscores this point by speaking to the Pharisees: when an evil spirit has gone out of a man, the person must not leave himself empty. If he does, the devil that had been sent out and is looking for an abode and finding none will return to the place it had left. And when it finds it empty and swept, it goes and brings along seven other spirits. And since they are now eight in number who have occupied the space, the person's last state will be worse than the first (Mt 12:43-45). Here, Jesus warns of the danger of just cleaning one's life and leaving it empty without filling it with God; the person leaves room for the devil to return. Scriptures provide a concrete record of this in the book of Ezra, where the people of Israel purged themselves of idolatry but failed to replace it with love for God and obedience to him. Ridding oneself of one's old ways is a first step towards a good life. We must also take the second step, which is to fill in the vacuum with the good of the gospel.[3] This is the rule of substitution in practice.

Our journey towards self-mastery requires applying the rule of substitution. The denunciation of any aspect of our weaknesses and untamed excesses is one good step. However, we must always take the second step to fill the space with something positive; oth-

---

[2] https://www.englishclub.com/ref/esl/Sayings/Quizzes/Mixed_2/Nature_abhors_a_vacuum_555.php. 17.06.2019.

[3] *Life Application Study Bible.* Illinois: Tyndale, 2007. p. 1714.

erwise, the denounced negative behaviour returns. And the last state may be worse. This rule of substitution is often used also as "replacement therapy" in helping addicts to overcome their conditions. Whenever a vice is removed, the space must be filled with virtue. It is a rule of nature; it abhors a vacuum.

Chapter 20

CONDUCT DEFENCE INSTINCT

"Master, I knew that you were a harsh man, reaping where you did not sow and gathering where you did not scatter seed; so I was afraid and went and hid your talent in the ground." (Matt. 25:24-25)

Nature has endowed all living things with a wonderful gift of self-preservation, also called the survival instinct. By means of it, each living creature has a built-in mechanism that engages anything that threatens its survival. This mechanism is found in humans as well as in animals, where the body produces antibodies to fight anything it senses as foreign. It is a reflex system in the body that does not consult with us before getting to work. Nature has designed it so that this system activates automatically as soon as it senses a threat or danger.[1]

This process not only operates internally in our bodies but also externally. For instance, it is the instinct of self-preservation that makes us sneeze when we inhale something strange to our bodies. The same instinct of self-preservation makes our eyelids blink to protect our eyes from perceived danger or to lubricate them against dryness. Also, when passing under an iron bar on the road in a car, the instinct of self-preservation makes us bend our heads even when the bar is far off above the car. The reaction is usually automatic, swift, and without consultation of the human rational facul-

[1] Merriam Webster Dictionary (Since 1828). https://www.merriam-webster Dictionary.com/dictionary/self-preservation.

ty. This instinct is good and beautiful for the preservation of our lives and protection against bodily harm.

The human brain has a similar capacity for thought. It can swiftly generate ideas for self-exoneration. Based on this capacity, some people have developed a defensive instinct in response to their aberrant conduct, stemming from their weaknesses and untamed excesses. They have trained themselves over time to the point that their brains and mouths have become programmed to generate and present swift, intuitive responses for every action. They insist on defending actions that are obviously morally indefensible. And since the intuition has been developed to the level that it has become their attitude, they act instinctively and effortlessly. In other words, a defence instinct develops from repeated defensive behaviours.[2] The attitude of the servant who received the one talent in the parable is a good representation of those with the conduct defence instinct (Matt. 25:24-25). Some are quick to remind those who draw their attention to any wrong they do to Jesus' teaching: "You shall not judge" (Matt. 7:1).

This attitude is highly inimical and antithetical to the struggle to attain self-mastery. The struggle requires openness to constructive criticism from those around us and to the guidance of wisdom for greater discernment. A person needs to be ready to appreciate those who criticise him constructively and to take time afterward to think deeply about their criticisms and process them, rather than always launching one's defence arsenal. Wisdom always guides us to realise if we have erred or not. This is necessary in

---

[2] https://www.britannica.com/topic/instinct/instinct-as-behaviour.

view of the fact that, due to human limitations, personal considerations can at times influence our actions, even when we deem them best in the moment of acting. There are also times when our actions stem from insufficient knowledge about a particular issue.

There is no doubt that, as rational beings, we do have our reasons and justifications for almost every action. And there is no harm in one being able to explain oneself. As a matter of fact, one is expected to stand one's ground when one is sure one is right and has acted with a clear conscience in accordance with the objective truth. However, one may not go on with insistence, defending an action that glaringly falls short of objectively discernible truths. No amount of power of oratory and rhetoric can baptise a wrong action into a good one. This attitude blocks the possibility of learning from past mistakes and charting a new course towards attaining self-mastery. This is the main weakness of the conduct defence instinct.

A person with the conduct defence instinct constantly works and walks directly against established known truths thereby making that person the measure of right or wrong. The conduct defence instinct is characteristic of egoism which views the goodness or badness of an action only from the point of view of one's interest.[3] It has a close connection to Hobbesian egoism, in which actions are propelled and justified by self-interest and considered necessary for survival. The defence instinct can be inconsistent, as the same person is likely to denounce the very action they once

---

[3] Rich Dempsey, https://econfaculty.gmu.edu/bcaplan/instinct2.

carried out and defended. The conduct defence instinct antagonises the struggle towards self-mastery.

Chapter 21

IN PRINCIPLE

"If you don't live for something, you will die for nothing." (Unknown)

We have seen that one thing that differentiates humans from other creatures is rationality. As rational beings, we are capable of setting for ourselves propositional parameters that guide our actions and utterances called principles. A principle can be defined as a "basic general truth" or a "guiding rule for personal behaviour".[1] It is also defined as a basic belief, theory, or rule that significantly influences how a person behaves.[2] Principles are internalised objective and positive personal values. A person who lives life in principle follows acceptable rules of conduct in life.[3] Principles are ideological; they are sets of convictions based on values. They are moral compasses.

Principles guide a person's choices. A principled person does not do what is not right or say what is not true. He avoids what would displease him if done to him. According to Marcus Aurelius, the guiding rule for a principled person is: "If it is not right, do not do it; if it is not true, do not say it"[4] (cf. Matt. 7:12). Principles are underlying parameters of truth from which a person bases his

---

[1] *Oxford Advanced Learner's Dictionary, 4th Edition.*

[2] *Macmillan English Dictionary for Advanced Learners, New Edition.*

[3] *Merriam-Webster, Since 1828.* www.merriam-webster.com. 16.02. 2020.

[4] https://www.brainyquote.com.

evaluation of issues and takes his decisions. Ray Dalio submits that principles allow one to live a life consistent with one's values. They connect a person's values to their actions.[5] Man moulds principles and they, in turn, mould man. A man must be sure that he is guided by an underlying principle upon which he makes every decision in life. Principles promote consistency.

Principles are indispensable vehicles by which an individual attains self-mastery. A person builds his character and integrity by being faithful to his principles. Principles polish a person's character. A person's behaviours are natural fallouts of his principles. An individual without principles is directionless; he lives for nothing and never develops. Samuel Smiles captures this point thus: "A man without principles and will is like a ship without a compass; it changes direction with every change of wind".[6] Hence, living without principles is like embarking on a journey without a destination.

The Christian life is built on basic principles, namely our beliefs, systems, and values. In formulating personal principles, Christians must adopt principles that respect both natural and divine laws. By natural law, we are talking about the natural ordering of things. By divine law, we refer to God's revelation of Himself to humanity. We come to know natural law through natural reason, while we know divine law through God's revelation of himself, which reaches its peak in Jesus Christ.

It is not just enough for a person to have principles. The person must live according to them. Principles are useless if they are formulated and not lived out. An individual must take responsibility

---

[5] Ibidem.

[6] Ibidem.

and ensure they keep their own principles; otherwise, they are nothing more than mere cosmetics. Principles are never to be compromised for affiliations, social acceptability, or other considerations. Living according to principles is not about personal convenience, as one's principles can be uncomfortable. A wise man once said, "If you are willing to abandon your principles for convenience or social acceptability, they are not principles, they are your costume."[7] Those who desire to live principled lives, therefore, need the courage to stand by their decision amid and against all odds. Personal adjustable principles may be updated or reviewed to meet emergent realities of life. They would, however, need not deviate from the objective truth or be manipulated to serve only personal convenience.

Acting in principle means acting according to right reason because every principle of life is expected to have been carefully thought out based on a positive value. In a complex world where sophistication breeds confusion, one needs principles to guide one through. One who lives according to principles builds their integrity even in a messy world. Nicolas Chamfort asserts that "A person without principles is devoid of character: if he had character, he would feel he needs principles".[8] A person who lives without principles acts without focus and can scarcely attain self-mastery. Principles define people's directions in life. Stephen Covey says, "There are three constants in life…change, choice, and principles."[9] There

---

[7] Ibidem.

[8] https://www.brainyquote.com.

[9] Ibidem.

is a saying that "If you don't live for something, you will die for nothing" (Unknown). According to Kim Atman, people who focus on and live by principles can transcend their egos and free themselves from the shackles of the rule of opinion and personal feelings. In other words, principles guard the individual against the tendency toward self-assertion and self-indulgence, and against the risk of becoming a victim of his own emotions and personal feelings.[10]

A person must set for himself principles based on the values of his convictions. It is common to see people become more concerned with the pursuit of wealth, money, fame, and power than with personal principles. Herche worries about this unfortunate situation where people often do not take much care in forming their guiding principles. Ralph Waldo Emerson expresses the apprehension that "A man is usually more careful of his money than he is of his principles".[11] Herche, therefore, recommends that each person build sets of principles that are solid and true.[12]

There may be general principles in the form of policies within the groups, communities, or societies to which one belongs. One, however, needs to cultivate one's personal principles. This is because personal principles enhance one's ability to adhere to the policies. A man does no good to himself if he is committed to developing principles for the public while he has none for himself.

---

[10] Kim Atman, "The Importance of Being 'Principle Centered'". www.teachingvalues.com.

[11] https://www.brainyquote.com.

[12] Katie Herche, "The Importance of Principles". www.principles.org.

Principles are life compasses for navigating the noisy, sophisticated, modern world we live in.

A life devoid of principle is simply a recipe for arbitrariness, which is invariably opposed to authentic human development and the attainment of self-mastery. Arbitrariness is a disregard for objectivity, in which choices and decisions are informed by considerations other than truth. Friendship, filial relationships, the quest for popularity or social acceptability, personal comfort, and material things could sway a mind that operates arbitrarily. Arbitrariness diminishes one's integrity, can bring about conflict, and breeds bitterness among community members, leading to failure. According to Jawaharlal Nehru, "Failure comes only when we forget our ideals and objectives and principles."[13]

There may be times when concrete experiences require flexibility. However, the flexibility should not compromise the principles. The flexibility could be the application of a particular principle in a given circumstance, to the extent that it respects and promotes human dignity and the common good. Even at this, it needs to be so formulated in accordance with the principles of common good and fairness that it could be applied to any other similar circumstance if it arises. The principle remains constant except when a review is needed, if it is reviewable. Anyone who gets flexible with his principles puts himself on a slippery path. Eleanor Roosevelt warns, "Be flexible, but stick to your principles."[14] According to Abraham Lincoln, "Important principles may, and must be inflexi-

[13] John Adamu, https://www.brainyquote.com.

[14] Adamu, 18.02.2020.

ble".[15] It is worth noting that a person who is inflexible in their principles may be unpopular. However, the person who is faithful to principles has their integrity secure. John Adamu, in "Brainyquote.com", insists on faithfulness to principles when he says, "Always stand on principle even if you stand alone".[16] It is better to stand alone than to compromise a person's character and integrity.

Wisdom, due discretion, and courage are needed in the formulation and application of principles. They are also needed to determine the extent to which to be flexible in applying a principle. For instance, Jesus would relax the law forbidding work when human life needs to be saved. He exhibited this when he healed the paralytic in the temple (John 5:1-17). On one occasion, the disciples got very hungry and plucked corn and ate on the Sabbath. The Pharisees accused Jesus of allowing them to do what was unlawful and forbidden on the Sabbath. Jesus told them the Sabbath was made for man (Mark 2:23-27). The Synagogue leaders expressed indignation over his healing on the Sabbath (Luke 13:10-16). Recall, however, that the same Jesus refused to give the Pharisees and the Sadducees a sign (Matt. 16:1-4). He also refused to take any of the offers of the devil at the temptation (Matt. 4:1-10).

A principled person may become an attraction to many. Four categories of people may seek his friendship. The first category consists of those who may believe that he can help them grow. Such people would want to be close to the principled person out of a sincere desire to develop and grow in the principles he embodies.

---

[15] Adamu, 18.02.2020.

[16] Adamu, 18.02.2020.

The second category consists of those who may wish to be friends with him just for the sake of it. Those in this category want to have a story to tell about being close to this principled person, who is the attraction to everyone. The third category consists of those who may be drawn to him purely out of admiration but may later begin working to get him to blend in with them by compromising his principles. This category may wish to arm-twist the principled person and reduce him to their own level of living. Upon coming close to the principled man, they may soon consider him too strict, mean, and lacking human feelings if he does not give in to their whims and caprices. What gives a person integrity and makes him a person of honour is "being principled," not pleasing people. The fourth group consists of those who may get close to him solely to test his integrity. This group aims to lure the principled person to see his level of commitment to his convictions. These kinds of friends want to know whether his being principled is genuine or fake.

A principled person usually loses many of his friends who were initially attracted to him but do not share his value orientation, especially if he is dead set on not aligning with them. The principled person is guided by the desire to do what is always right, not by the desire to be correct. Seeking to do what is right means seeking to conform to objective truth, whereas seeking to do what is correct could mean seeking to conform to a particular person's or people's set standards and expectations. It is better to be alone than to compromise one's principles for friendship. Once a person begins to compromise his own principles, he compromises his character and integrity and soon runs bankrupt. And if this happens, those same friends for whom he compromised his principles will change and join in stoning him. It is, therefore, good to be principled and consistently so, because it is the sure path for attaining self-mastery.

Chapter 22

ABILITY FOR SELF-DIALOGUE

"In everything a prudent man acts with knowledge, but a fool flaunts his folly." (Prov. 13:16)

Self-dialogue is the ability to converse with oneself. It is an interaction of a person with himself. With this ability, a person talks to himself about what concerns him. Victor Shaw explains that self-dialogue involves a constant process of interaction between "I" and "me".[1] The object of self-dialogue is to ensure better self-management. According to Shaw, it serves as an adaptive mechanism for self-presentation, identity acquisition, stress management, health maintenance, and personal integration.[2] Self-dialogue is also called self-talk, inner speech, and inner discourse. It is important in planning, problem solving, self-reflection, self- image, critical thinking, self- inspection, self- criticism,[3] etc.

Self-dialogue is the internal dialogue of one's thoughts, a voice in one's head that comments on one's life.[4] After God, your next best counsellor is you. This is because, apart from God, no one understands what goes on in a person better than himself. In his infinite wisdom, God endowed each of us with this capacity. It is in-

---

[1] Victor N. Shaw, "Self-Dialogue as a Fundamental Process of Expression" in *JSTOR*. https://www.jstor.org.

[2] Ibid.

[3] "Internal Monologue". www.en.m.wikipedia.org

[4] "Managing Your Internal Dialogue". www.skillsyouneed.com.

nate in each of us; we are born with it, and we die with it. No one takes it from us. Each person must, therefore, activate this God-given capacity and put it to positive use.

The capacity for self-dialogue encompasses the capacity to learn and to discern. One can gain knowledge on one's own through personal experiences, those of others, or other channels where experiences are deposited. By putting together the knowledge from these experiences, one can advise oneself and make good decisions. Through self-dialogue, one positively engages with oneself to become a better person.

This innate capacity in each one of us is waiting to be developed. However, some people hardly even realise they have such a great capacity. Others have had this capacity either crushed, disabled, or replaced by an inferiority mindset. By this, they have either completely lost or partially lost confidence in their ability to engage in self-dialogue. Some have also not come to a realisation of it, thereby functioning without recognising it. Each person needs to activate this wonderful God-given innate capacity.

The capacity of self-dialogue is natural in each human being and constitutes a right. This right is an entitlement that does not need to be denigrated by a group or community. What the community owes the individual is assistance in developing this capacity and principles that strengthen it so it functions at its best.

Self-dialogue leads to self-counsel. It is a capacity in a human being to generate ideas to address matters arising in his life. After reflecting on an issue and weighing its pros and cons, one advises oneself on the appropriate steps to take. When a person discovers that he has erred, he reprimands, cautions, and counsels himself to do better in the future. On the journey of growth and maturity in life, one needs to engage in self-dialogue. Self-dialogue is indispensable in the struggle towards attaining self-mastery.

Chapter 23

SELF-REPROACH CAPACITY

"Let us test and examine our ways." (Lam. 3:40)

The journey towards the attainment of self-mastery requires engaging in self-reproach. The capacity for self-reproach is necessary for human development and the struggle to attain self-mastery. Reproach means to charge with blame for something wrong; to rebuke. It is an expression of disapproval or an expression of displeasure. Self-reproach means blame, rebuke, or expression of disapproval or displeasure; it means to criticise oneself. Self-reproach is when a person holds himself responsible for his wrongdoing.[1] It is an internal dialogue, a self-interrogation that takes place within a person's inner self. Self-reproach requires great humility, for no one who rides the horse of pride can engage in it. It requires an honest acceptance of one's imperfection. As a matter of fact, self-reproach is an act of the imperfect. Anyone with the slightest drop of imagination of perfection cannot indulge in self-reproach but rather in self-praise.

The ability and courage to engage in self-reproach are noble. It is a demonstration of honesty with oneself and not being egocentric. The ability to interrogate and caution oneself regarding something wrong one has done or said, to blame, rebuke, and caution oneself, is an exhibition of great audacity. Self-reproach involves

---

[1] https://www.merriam-webster.com/thesaurus/self-reproach.

focusing on oneself, scrutinising oneself, and apportioning blame or praise as the case may require. It is the ability to look back on one's conduct and criticise oneself.

A playback of one's life is necessary at intervals, as far as the struggle to attain self-mastery is concerned. It was Socrates, the ancient father of philosophy, who once remarked that an unexamined life is not worth living.[2] Observably, some fear journeying into their inner selves. They fear facing the "skeletons" of their hearts. Such people develop headaches and goosebumps whenever they attempt to face their inner selves. However, the same people can reproach others over their mistakes. The people in this category hardly apply that same amount of energy to themselves, either. Through self-reproach, a person can make the necessary corrections and behavioural adjustments, find peace, and achieve self-mastery. Through self-reproach, one can, at least in imagination, feel what others feel when one reproaches them. Since no one will harshly reproach himself, the person learns how to reproach others with compassion.

The lack of ability and courage to look inward is a major hindrance to self-reproach and, consequently, a stumbling block to the attainment of self-mastery. Realistically, it is much easier to indulge in self-praise than in self-reproach. It is still easier if the self-reproach is done collectively than individually. In collective self-reproach, a person blames himself along with others. Our human nature pulls us to sin. We must develop the ability and courage to

---

[2] https://www.google.com/amp/s/schoolworkhelper.net.

engage in self-reproach. No matter what, we must be determined to move on. That is the path of self-mastery.

The purpose of embarking on self-reproach is to enable one to see where one went wrong, to correct oneself and make resolutions on how to avoid such wrong action in due course. Self-reproach helps a person who has erred to retrace his way. It helps a person who has committed an error to realise his wrong and make a U-turn. Decisions taken at a personal level after self-reproach are by far more effective because they are resolutions taken after the pain of self-blame and regret. The purpose of self-reproach is not self-condemnation. It is rather aimed at focusing on one's imperfections, denouncing them, asking for forgiveness, and charting a new course. It is a stepladder by which one climbs above one's imperfections. Self-reproach should not be confused with being scrupulous. A scrupulous person is one who feels, accommodates, and entertains guilt over actions, of commission or omission, which do not amount to sin.[3] A scrupulous person continues to feel the guilt of a sin even after he has been forgiven.

There are instances of people who stand out in the attitude of self-reproach in the Bible. Pharaoh reproached himself before Moses and Aaron (Exo. 9:27). Job reproached himself for his thoughts (7:10; 33:27). King Saul confessed that he had sinned (1 Sam. 15:24; 15:30). King David is an outstanding biblical figure for his humility and attitude of self-reproach. He constantly reproaches himself and asks God for pardon. After the Prophet Nathan had disclosed to David how he committed adultery with Uriah's wife and later

---

[3] Heribert Jone, *Moral Theology*. Illinois: TAN, 1993. p. 39.

murdered him, David reproached himself and confessed; "I have sinned against the Lord" (2 Sam. 12:13). David's heart troubled him after he had numbered the people and he confessed in self-reproach; "I have sinned greatly in what I have done" (2 Sam. 24:10). In Psalm 41:4, David prays; "O Lord, be gracious to me; Heal me, for I have sinned against you." The most glaring of David's acts of self-reproach is in Psalm 51. He states categorically in vv. 3-4: "For I know my transgressions and my sin is ever before me. Against you, you alone, have I sinned, and done evil in your sight". King Hezekiah followed this noble example of David when he acknowledged his wrongdoing toward the Assyrian King (2 Kings 18:14). Judas Iscariot made a self-reproach for betraying his innocent master (Matt. 27:4). Unfortunately, he did not go beyond his self-reproach to seek forgiveness. Consequently, he slid into hopelessness and committed suicide.

Self-reproach basically involves five things. First, there is the feeling of being sorry for the wrong that has been done. Second, there is the seeking of forgiveness. This is when one admits one's wrong before God or anyone one has offended and seeks reconciliation. It is also important to accept forgiveness when forgiven and to forgive oneself. Third, there is a resolve to avoid falling into the same wrong. Fourth is the prayer for strength to be faithful to one's resolve not to fall back to the same wrong again. Fifth is the constant reading of the Holy Scriptures, which keeps us connected with God. A person struggling to attain self-mastery must realise, activate, and utilise the capacity for self-reproach by which he can conduct an honest scrutiny of himself. We must each test and examine our ways (Lam. 3:40).

Chapter 24

VERDICT OF TRUTH

"Do not judge, and you will not be judged." (Matt. 7:1)

The teaching of Jesus, "Do not judge, and you will not be judged" (Matt. 7:1), has become a topical subject of discourse. Some use this teaching defensively as a shield against correction and caution. They claim they are being judged against Jesus' injunction. Thus, a good number of Christians hold back when there is the need to correct erring brothers and sisters lest they be accused of being judgemental. Even some spouses find it difficult to correct their partners lest they be accused of being judgemental. This is also the case between some parents and children, and among some friends.[1]

Those who believe that correcting or cautioning them when they err means judgement often react aggressively towards anyone who makes an effort to correct or caution them. This has become a strategy by which some people chicken people around them so that they can do whatever they wish without being challenged. They use the "Do not judge" to shield their weaknesses and untamed excesses. Some pertinent questions seek answers here. Does our Lord's command not to judge mean that truth should not be told an errant person? Does it imply that Christians do not have a moral obligation to correct in love those who err or sin? What about the

[1] https://bible.org/seriespage.

demand of Christ that we should be our brother's keeper? Is this a correct understanding of our Lord's command, "Do not judge"? Does this understanding not promote Christian moral indifference? Does their understanding not constitute blackmail against the voice of truth?

The Holy Scriptures admonish Christians to correct one another in mutual love. This includes even those who engage us in fruitless doctrinal arguments (Tim. 2:23-26). St. Paul opposed Peter publicly for compromising his convictions. St. Peter had openly stated that circumcision was not necessary for salvation. Therefore, there was no need to put its yoke on the gentile (Acts 15). Also, he taught that Gentiles were not to be discriminated against for not being circumcised. True to his conviction, Peter ate with the uncircumcised at Antioch. However, upon the arrival of some circumcised persons, Peter drew back and separated himself from the uncircumcised for fear of the circumcised party. For acting this drama, St. Paul reacted thus: "I opposed him to his face, because he stood condemned" (Gal. 2:11-14).

The Christian life is governed by beliefs that include "dos" and "don'ts" expressed in the form of aphorisms, commands, exhortations, etc. At this point, the Ten Commandments come to mind as foundational moral norms for Christians and Christ's teaching. They are not abrogated by the Lord's teaching on "Do not judge". He teaches, "Think not that I have come to abolish the law and the prophets; I have come not to abolish them but to fulfil them" (Matt. 5:17). To the young man who wished to enter eternal life, our Lord instructed him to keep the commandments (Matt. 19:16-10). Therefore, the Ten Commandments and other numerous precepts of Holy Scriptures, including those defined by the Church under the guidance of the Holy Spirit, are divine truths. And God expects Christians to believe and live by them. A deliberate and wilful violation of any of those divine truths constitutes disobedience towards their giver: God.

On the strength of this understanding of the commandments and all other divine precepts, it means that truth by its very nature is a judge. A choice from options and the determination of what is the truth automatically implies a judgement on the other variables. Acting against any of these truths sets the violator against the particular truth violated. Consequently, the violation attracts the judgement of the particular truth on the violator. This is an inescapable reality.

Hence, truth itself is a judge. This truth is fully expressed in Scripture, which says that the Word of God has the power to judge even the secret thoughts of men and women (Heb. 4:12). Therefore, whenever there is a violation, the only way out is for the violator to repent, seek forgiveness, and make amends. The gentle corrective voice of a brother or sister should, hence, be seen only as an expression of love towards the errant person. The one correcting the errant person is to be seen as an intermediary and facilitator of reconciliation between the errant person and truth. Jesus Christ is the personification of truth (John 14:6). A violation of a divine truth is therefore invariably a disrespect of Jesus Christ, who is truth itself.

In common usage, "to judge" means to decide a case in a law court by a public officer vested with the legal authority to do so.[2] It means to hear and determine in an official capacity the merits of a case or the guilt of a person.[3] Being judgemental involves the willingness to criticise other people's actions and behaviours and to say they are wrong.[4] What then does the prohibition "Do not judge" mean? The prohibition means any attempt to wash ourselves clean while condemning others and concluding that they cannot enter the kingdom of heaven.[5] It forbids self-exoneration while viewing others as convicts. He forbids discrimination and the outright rejection of people for having erred. It forbids having "A censorious attitude towards others".[6]

A judgemental attitude is exemplified in the attitude of the Pharisee towards the tax collector as expressed in his prayer (Luke 18:9-14). He claims all the righteousness while denouncing the tax collector. He praises himself and slams the tax collector. He washes himself clean before God and condemns the tax collector. He gives good reasons why God should receive his prayer and reject the tax collector's. He exalts himself and humbles the tax collector. He condemns and despises the tax collector and goes on to give God reason to do the same. The Pharisee indicts the tax collector and

---

[2] *Oxford Advanced Learner's Dictionary.* Fourth Edition, 1989.

[3] *The New International Webster's Comprehensive Dictionary of English Language.*2004 Edition. Print.

[4]*Macmillan English Dictionary for Advanced Learner sedition.* Print.

[5] *The International Bible Commentary* (Bangalore: Theological). Commentary on Matthew 7:1.

[6] *The New Bible Commentary: Revised* (England: Inter- Varsity1977) Commentary on Matthew 7:1. Print.

discriminates against him because he sees him as a bad person. This is very different from an honest act of fraternal correction done out of mutual love.

Also, our Lord's prohibition, "Do not judge", is a prohibition against rash judgement. This means to assume as true, even tacitly, the moral fault of a neighbour without sufficient foundation.[7] Rash judgement is the act of deducing, by assumption, negative meanings from a neighbour's thoughts, words, and deeds without an effort to get clarification from the neighbour. It involves the presumptuous injection of interpretations into another person's thoughts, words, and deeds. Drawing a conclusion over someone's thoughts, words, and deeds, and holding such a conclusion against the person based on mere suspicion is rash judgement.[8]

From the foregoing, it is obvious that what distinguishes fraternal correction from judgment is the motive and manner in which the correction is done. It amounts to a clear misunderstanding and a blatant misinterpretation of our Lord's teaching by those who label anyone who approaches them to offer them corrections as judging them. Jesus did not intend his teaching to be used as a cheap blackmail against being corrected. Those who set out to correct the errant must do it out of love. They need to convince the errant person that they care about him. Fraternal correction also requires wisdom. Therefore, the exhortation, 'not to judge,' by no means implies compromising truth.

---

[7] CCC, no. 2477.

[8] Brian Mullady, "Questions Answered" (https://www.hprweb.com/2018/07/questions-answered-64/

The one correcting must ensure he prays for what he prepares to undertake, prays for the errant person, and thinks deeply about the argument he will present to convince the errant person. Wisdom demands that the manner of talking to the errant person is persuasive rather than accusative. Correction must not be confrontational or quarrelsome. Correction should not be antagonistic but charitable, affectionate, and in an atmosphere of friendship. Other dispositions needed in mutual correction include gentleness, kindness, patience, and perseverance. The one correcting should use the word of God as the basis for his argument and avoid sounding too personal. This is how to correct an errant person without being judgemental.

Fraternal and mutual correction is necessary in the struggle to attain self-mastery. The people correcting us help us see what we may not have seen, overlooked, or taken for granted. Mutual correction is not judgement. Jesus would not want us to vindicate ourselves while denouncing others for the same conduct we are guilty of. Jesus would want us to be our brothers' keepers by mutual correction. However, those being corrected need to accept the corrections in good faith, as they do not amount to judgment. Fraternal and mutual correction is key to attaining self-mastery.

Chapter 25

THE JOHARI WINDOW IMPORT

"Those who trust in their own wits [alone] are fools".
(Prov. 28:26)

The struggle to attain self-mastery is complex. It involves both the efforts of the individual and of others around him through available feedback mechanisms. The individual must avoid the error of thinking he knows everything about himself. He needs to come to terms with the reality that everyone has blind spots in their lives. These are things which a person does not know about himself but are seen only by others. The person can learn this only by opening up to honest feedback. It does a person much good to get feedback to help him identify his areas of strength to improve on and his weaknesses to work on. This is where I find the Johari window theory relevant in the journey towards self-mastery.

The Johari window theory is a quadrant model that helps people gain a better understanding of their communication and interactions with others, fostering understanding and stronger relationships. The Johari window theory was created by Joseph Luft and Harrington Ingham in 1955. This model enhances perception through two thrusts of ideas. It has to do with revealing information about you to others and learning from their feedback. The theory derives its name from the first names of the duo, Joseph and

Harrington.[1] The quadrants of the Johari Window, or arenas as they are also called, are: the open space, the blind spot, the hidden area, and the unknown area.[2] They are called four window perspectives. This theory does not originally have a theological slant. The theological input is achieved by bringing God into the knowledge variables, since the Christian believes that God is all-knowing.

The first arena is the open arena. This is the open self. It comprises the behaviours, feelings and emotions of the person that are known to God, to the person and to other members of one's group. In this arena, people get to know the person through interactions with the person and with members of the group. The second arena is the blind spot, also called the blind self. This is the arena in which certain information about a person's personality is known to God and to others but not known to the person. It could be certain talents in a person that only others can see. However, members of a person's group may have a particular perception and interpretation of a person's behaviours that may not be entirely accurate. Someone wallowing in ideologies that exonerate human weaknesses and untamed excesses may give faulty feedback. A person could be doing certain things with the best intentions and in good faith, but members of the group may perceive them negatively. The person can only learn about it from their feedback.[3] Care must be taken, however, that a person does not give in to subjective notions and

---

[1] "The Johari Window Model Theory". https://communication-theory.org/the-johari-window-model/.

[2] Ibid.

[3] https://www.toppr.com/guides/business-communication-and-ethics/intro-to-business-communication/johari-window/.

interactions not founded on sound convictions, objective principles, and truths.

Third is the hidden arena, also known as the façade. This is information that is known only to God and the person. This can be any personal information that the person wishes to keep or is reluctant to reveal. These include feelings, past experiences or plans, fears, and a person's top secrets. This information can only be known to any members of the group if the person decides to reveal it. A fourth arena is the unknown area or the unknown self. In this area, information about the person is unknown to the person and others. This area is known by God alone. It is only God who knows every person even before the person is formed in his mother's womb (Jer. 1:5) and what will happen in the future. This includes certain feelings, unexplored talents, and capabilities. The only way to know anything in this arena is through exploration and experimentation.[4]

The Johari Window theory confirms the limitations of each person's knowledge of himself. It reveals that those who pride themselves on claiming they know everything about themselves, in truth, know only a fraction. One can learn much from relations, friends, and associates in the groups to which one belongs. Therefore, the struggle towards self-mastery requires openness to this reality and a disposition to accept feedback in humility and use it positively.

A person who is determined to conquer himself needs a great deal of self-awareness and insight into his personality. Part of the

---

[4] Ibid.

assessment in the journey of self-conquest includes feedback from acquaintances. The Johari window theory is a wonderful technique for obtaining this feedback, which the person can subsequently use to improve their awareness of themselves and others. It helps in understanding one's relationship with oneself, with God, and with others. A person who has no healthy relationship with himself can rarely have a good relationship with God and/or with others.

His character defines every human being. And a person's character is what bears testimony of his person to others. A person's character is an aggregate of values appropriated by the individual from his growing environment, religion, and other values in the process of growth. Some of these values may have objective or subjective characters. Meanwhile, a person brought up with subjective values believes them to be the ultimate and has patterned his character accordingly. He will see no fault in his conduct. Such a person will experience a clash of values when he meets objective values through feedback. In this case, the person might begin to feel that others do not like him. Knowledge of the Johari Window feedback system and its integration is therefore of great significance and usefulness in the struggle to attain self-mastery.

Chapter 26

ILLUSORY TRUTH EFFECT

"Do not conform to this world, but be transformed by the renewal of your mind, that you may prove what is the will of God that is good and acceptable and perfect".
(Rom. 12:20)

There is power in repetition. The human mind has a built-in tendency to settle for what it hears repeatedly as being truthful. Many successful leaders use it. As a matter of fact, the power of repetition is the best friend of any good leader. They say one thing repeatedly.[1] Parents, teachers, preachers, and activists use this strategy positively. They sound an idea repeatedly until it gains acceptance or is at least tolerated.

According to Remez Sasson, thoughts are visitors to the mind. They visit the central station of the mind. They come, stay a while, and disappear to give space for other thoughts. Meanwhile, these thoughts are a mixture of words, sentences, mental images, and sensations. Some thoughts linger, gain power, and affect the life of the person thinking them.[2] This is what manifests in human actions, positive or negative. If the thoughts occupying the mind are

---

1 https://getlighthouse.com/blog/power-of-repetition-successful-leaders.

2 Remez Sasson. https://www.successconsciousness.com/index_00004b.htm.

positive, they produce positive actions. If they are negative, however, they produce negative actions.[3]

M. Farouk Radwan is a psychologist who further explains one of the rules of the mind. The belief it holds tends to grow stronger with repetition, whether through listening, reading, or watching visuals.[4] Sasson gives an example: "Supposing you bought a new shirt, then a friend of yours told you that it looks good. What will happen if, later on, another friend tells you the same? The belief that the shirt is nice will grow stronger."[5] even if the shirt was not as good as your friends may have made it sound. Similarly, when the same friends repeatedly tell you that the same shirt is not good, there is a tendency that your feeling of the shirt being bad will get stronger.

The illusory truth effect refers to the impact that a well-packaged falsehood can have on the human psyche, gradually leading it to perceive the falsehood as true. Emily Dreyfuss explains that the illusory truth effect is a business strategy in which a lie can be made to seem like the truth. It leads one to believe a thing is what it is not. This strategy is very simple; say it again, and again, and again,[6] and you will see that many who had no interest in a thing may change their minds. Many marketers use the power of repetition to exploit the "illusory truth effect" as a strategy for mar-

---

[3] Sasson, 07.12.2019.

[4] Sasson, 07.12.2019.

[5] Sasson, 07.12.2019.

[6] Emily Dreyfuss, https://www.wired.com/2017/02/dont-believe-lies-just-prople-people-repeat/amp.

keting their products.[7] Those packaging adverts use this business strategy to the fullest. For instance, although tobacco smoking is dangerous to health, the repeated play of its beautifully packaged advert attracts some youths. In the same way, promoters of ideologies also celebrate weaknesses and untamed excesses.

By the illusory truth effect strategy, a marketer could make you buy something that you may not need. There is the story of a man who came back from the market with crutches in the boot of his car. Back home, he was asked why he had bought them, since he didn't have any issues with his legs. His surprising response was that he didn't even know why he'd bought them. He said that the boy selling them just convinced him to buy it. This is an example of how the illusory truth effect makes a thing plausible and eventually attractive.

The illusory truth effect strategy is manipulative used not only by marketers but also by politicians. They are big-time experts at using it. They use it in their campaigns and propaganda as a selling point to present themselves as more competent than their opponents. In reality, the person being packaged and marketed may actually be very incompetent. What the strategy does is create a cognitive bias so that the person eventually comes to believe something that is false.

Dreyfuss explains that the illusory truth effect strategy works because there is a glitch in the human psyche that tends to equate repetition with truth. Therefore, the more a thing is repeated over and over and over, the more a person begins to equate it with truth.

---

[7] Dreyfuss, 07.12.2019.

This is how repeated exposure to the same fake news can make a person begin to feel as if there is something truthful about the story. What is believed to be wrong, false, or unacceptable gradually gets to be believed to be right, true, and acceptable. This glitch is due to human imperfection.[8] Most of the biases we develop against some people stem from the illusory truth effect. At first, we do not believe what we are being told about the person. Later, we gradually begin to tolerate it and eventually settle for it, no matter how little the degree of settlement may be. This is what happens with a person who dwells on theories that exonerate human weaknesses and untamed excesses.

Promoters of immoral ideologies like abortion, gay marriage, masturbation, contraception, exaggerated senses of freedom, belief in the absolute autonomy of the human person, etc., also use the illusory truth effect strategy. This strategy can also be used to corrupt a person's sense of guilt by repeatedly making the person feel that there is nothing wrong with such an act. A person gradually comes to feel okay about things they used to feel guilty about, like aberrant actions stemming from one's weaknesses and untamed excesses. The illusory truth effect strategy is quite simple but a very powerful, pervasive strategy that only a person with a very clear sense of judgment can withstand. The strategy can make the most learned person docile to a near illiterate person.

A person struggling to attain self-mastery must beware of the illusory truth effect. This is because the person will surely encounter promoters of ideologies inimical to the perfection he is pursu-

---

[8] Dreyfuss, 07.12.2019.

ing – mediocre ideas that feel at home with human weaknesses and untamed excesses. Such ideologies can sway him off track. The salvation of a person against the illusory truth effect is the adoption of a principled life. Principles help a person on the journey towards self-mastery to make good choices. One needs to be careful about the tendency to move with the trends, as those obsessed with new things could easily fall for the illusory truth effect.

It is to be noted that the illusory truth effect strategy could catch up with one through a gradual process. Usually, when a person hears new information, they compare it with existing credible sources to ascertain its truthfulness. However, researchers have found that familiarity, which comes from repeated exposure to the same thing, can trump rationality, leading to paradoxical feelings about a known wrong. Constant hearing could make a person start to feel as if something is right.[9] The illusory truth effect strategy is a shrewd process that passes from indignation to tolerance, then to attraction, and finally to acceptance.

Our initial reaction when we hear a lie being branded as truth is indignation. This is an angry reaction to the wrong thing a person has heard, which is painted as right. After repeatedly listening to the same thing, a person begins to develop a measure of tolerance for the falsehood. And this tolerance increases with repeated listening. As the tolerance level increases, the false information begins to sound appealing, attracting the person to listen to it. By now, the person is just a few steps away from accepting the same

[9] Dreyfuss, 07.12.2019.

false information as being true. This is especially true of faint-hearted persons.

The illusory truth effect is particularly dangerous in the struggle to attain self-mastery because it can make a person feel okay with his weaknesses and untamed excesses. It could gradually lead a faint-hearted person to conform to ideologies inimical to Christian values, thereby sabotaging the journey towards self-mastery. This is why the person struggling to attain self-mastery must make the deliberate choice to be guided by sound principles and convictions and never allow himself to get swindled by the illusory truth effect. Christians must, therefore, develop the habit of always reading the Holy Bible, as it is the treasure trove of Christian values and principles.

Chapter 27

THE HOMING TENDENCY

"Then he goes and brings with him seven other spirits more evil than himself, and they enter and dwell there; and the last state of that man shall become worse than the first." (Matt. 12:45)

Flor McCarthy gives an interesting description of the homing instinct. It means being able to return home, usually from a great distance.[1] Many animals have this instinct—for example, dogs, cats, pigs, goats, pigeons, etc. McCarthy gives the example of a Manx shearwater that was caught and ringed in Wales and taken to Boston, three thousand miles away, where it was released. The bird returned to the exact spot it was captured in Wales.[2] Human beings are not free from the homing instinct.

According to Flor McCarthy, homing is also found in humans.[3] He also points out that this instinct is generally a positive factor in human life.[4] Among Africans, for instance, the positive homing instinct manifests as a desire to connect with home, or at least their roots. No matter how educated, rich, and powerful they become, they never stop desiring to return to their old ancestral roots. As a sitting American president, Barack Obama visited Kenya and

---

[1] https://www.dictionary.com/browse/homing.

[2] Flor McCarthy, *New Sunday and Holyday Liturgies Year C.* Dublin: Dominican, 2000), 307.

[3] McCarthy, 307.

[4] McCarthy, 308.

traced his roots after long years in the US[5]. It was a historic and emotional event for both Obama and the Kenyan nation. Also, an African wrestling superstar from Ghana and then Smackdown Champion, Kofi Kingston, visited his home 26 years after he left for the US in pursuit of his dream in the wrestling profession.[6]

This homing instinct is not only physical but also attitudinal, manifesting in a person's tendencies. This is often where the negative homing instinct manifests. Humans tend to desire to return to their old selves. The homing instinct is a strong drive that keeps pulling the human being back to his old ways. Different people express this reality of homing in different ways. Hence, we have expressions such as "old habits never die," "you cannot teach an old monkey a new trick," and "you cannot erase the designs on a Zebra." What all these mean is that habits of a lifetime, good or bad, are difficult to change.[7] This idea does not contradict the belief that every human being has the capacity to change for better or worse at any stage of life. It only states the obvious: there is a tendency to slip back into the old. The situation can be likened to a tree in the wind. A straight tree will always return to its position, no matter how much the wind bends it. Similarly, a bent tree will return to its bent state no matter how the wind straightens it.[8] Except for the grace of God, human beings can easily slip back into their old atti-

---

[5] Josy Forsdike, https://www.theguardian.com/us-news/galary/2015/jul/25/....

[6] Ismail Akwei, https://face2faceafrica.com/article/wwe-star-kofi-kingston-returns-home-to-ghana-after-26-years-hotos.

[7] McCarthy, 307.

[8] McCarthy, 308.

tudes and behaviours. This is because there is something in their nature that propels them to behave in that same pattern despite being created in the image of God and redeemed by Christ. It takes the grace of God and a concerted struggle for a Christian to conquer his old self and live the new life of the redeemed (2 Cor. 5:17).

The homing tendency is best described by the term recidivism, from the Latin recidivus, literally meaning "a falling back," usually into bad habits. This was why Jesus admonished the woman caught in adultery when he told her to go and sin no more (John 8:11). He admonishes anyone who has been liberated to make sure he avoids relapsing because the latter state will be worse than the initial situation (Matt. 12:45). Jesus knew that it is very easy to slip into old bad habits. Every Christian needs to be aware of this, especially in the struggle towards attaining mastery over oneself. A fall-back in this struggle can be a serious setback.

The homing instinct is exemplified in the life of the biblical figure Gomer, daughter of Dibliaim. She lived a life of whoredom before God directed the Prophet Hosea to go and take her as his wife (Hosea 1:2). After getting married and bearing three children (Jezreel, Loruhama, and Loammi), she returned to her old life of whoredom (2:5). Many times, God directed Hosea to go after his wife and bring her back to his loving arms. She often returned to her old life. In his book The Confessions, St. Augustine recounts his struggles with strong temptations to return to his old ways. He narrates how sexual images of his past life survived. He explained that, as former habits, they were imprinted in his memory and played out suggestively to him while he was awake. The images also played out so strongly in dreams and even had the power of arousing him not only to pleasurable sensation, but to consent. According to St. Augustine, he struggled hard and, with God's help, resisted these temptations when he awoke.[9]

Seth J. Gillian is a psychologist who notes that it is very easy to slip back into discarded habits. He explains that the struggle to become a better person involves making the right decisions, following the right path, and avoiding those that do not. Making the right decisions is not a once-and-for-all endeavour. There is a strong temptation for us to assume that we have traveled so far away from those habits we have discarded, while in the real sense, they run alongside us.[10]

Gillian strongly cautions that we must avoid the "home free" or the "I have arrived " feeling and have our eyes continuously fixed on the struggle to self-mastery. In this light, he reveals certain dangerous deceptions one must not accommodate. First, no one should become overconfident that they have succeeded and imagine they can never return to their old ways. This impression is likely to form when a person has been on the right track for a while. A person may begin to feel that they are miles away from their bad habits and hence, immune to going back. Second, one must not entertain the feeling that one can bend the rules a little and still be ok. This feeling makes a person so confident that he can step in and out of them again without their getting a hold on him anymore. For instance, a person who has reasonably recovered from

---

[9] St. Augustine, *The Confessions* (Part I, vol. 1). New York: Augustinian Heritage Institute, 1997. P. 264.

[10] Seth J. Gillian, https://www.psychologytoday.com/us/blog/think-act-be/201511....

addiction may feel that he can have one bottle of beer, thinking it will not bring back his addiction.[11]

In the struggle towards self-mastery, therefore, care needs to be taken to form positive habits and remain committed to them to the end. Our conversion did not destroy our humanity with its weaknesses. Hence, we have a battle to engage in, to conquer it, if we wish to attain self-mastery. The effort needs to be sustained and never to relent or be compromised at any point. It is fatal to begin and fall back out of sheer carelessness. Hence, Gillian suggests ways to remain on track. Firstly, one needs to be mindful of one's urges. There are suggestive urges towards returning to what we have discarded. Consciousness of these urges helps us to be careful and reaffirm our commitment. Secondly, it is good to pay serious attention to anything that will suggest a return to one's old behaviours, e.g., the return of a flirting partner or an ex-smoker seeking employment in a tobacco company. Thirdly, there is a need to watch "permission-giving" thoughts that appraise us for doing well and are capable of luring us into making an ill-advised U-turn, e.g., thoughts like I can keep ice cream in the freezer without eating it, knowing full well that I tend to finish a quarter of a container in one night. Fourthly, be careful of sons and daughters of encouragement who have no idea what you are struggling to achieve, e.g., friends who will try to encourage you to drink more at an outing by convincing you that you don't have a drinking problem.[12]

Admittedly, habits are hard to break. If, however, a person has succeeded in breaking any, he needs to sustain the momentum to

---

[11] Gillian, 05.12.2019.

[12] Gillian, 05.12.2019.

avoid a fall-back called homing or *recidivism.* As much as it is important to try hard to avoid the homing tendency, it should be said that one can always start afresh with the hope of still making steady progress, even though the fallback would have led the person to register a certain degree of retrogression. There should, however, be no room for hopelessness and giving up in the struggle towards self-mastery. The struggle must be sustained to the end because once the hand has been laid on the plow, there is no looking back (Luke 9:62).

Chapter 28

FORMATION TERMINUS

"If you gathered nothing in your youth, how can you find something in your old age?" (Prov. 22:6)

No doubt, the process of human growth and development is a lifelong endeavour, and each person has the capacity to change for better or worse, though not always easily. Hence, this book consistently maintains that the pursuit of self-mastery is a lifelong endeavour. However, there is a striking reality to note, which can be referred to as the formation terminus. There comes a period in a person's life when the ability to change character becomes much more difficult. At a certain stage in life, a person becomes hardened and set, unable to adopt new behaviours readily.[1] Such an age comes with difficulty in behavioural adjustment because impediments to flexibility begin to set in. The ability for self-formation is limited. This is what I refer to as formation terminus. When a person reaches this formation terminus, the struggle to attain self-mastery becomes somewhat or very difficult, depending on the person, since it requires constant behavioural changes. This means that it is best to begin the journey towards self-mastery at a much younger age and pursue it vigorously. However, the journey can be embarked on at any age, trusting in God's gracious assistance.

[1] McCarthy, 307.

Science provides insight into why behavioural or habitual change is difficult at a later age. They have divided a person's journey of personality growth into two phases. The first phase spans from age zero to around age thirty, while the second phase spans from around age thirty to death. In the first phase, the likelihood of personality and behavioural adjustments in most people is quite high. Adjustments are much more difficult in the second phase. People are much more flexible and receptive in the first phase than in the second. Hence, in some people, behavioural and habitual change is possible with much greater relative ease in the first phase than in the second.

A renowned Harvard psychologist, William James, was the first to bring this theory to public attention in his 1890 publication, The Principles of Psychology. James revealed that, "In most of us, by the age of thirty, the character has set like plaster, and will never soften again".[2] Some other psychologists later critically questioned the veracity of this notion. In the end, however, many came to acknowledge that there is some truth to James's notion.

Occupational psychologist, Kirsten Godfrey, differentiates between a person's personality and their moods. Personality is a relatively stable set of patterns of thoughts, feelings, and behaviours, whereas moods are much more temporary.[3] She then states that personality development reaches a peak of stability from the age

---

[2] Rachel Hosie, "Is it Possible to Change Your Personality Past the Age of 30?" www.independent.co.uk.

[3] Hosie, 19.05.2020.

following adolescence into the early mid-twenties. So, to some extent, by the time one is thirty, one's personality is fully formed.[4]

David Buss, a professor of psychology at the University of Texas, posits that personality traits tend to remain very stable over time, particularly from age 30 onward.[5] Around this age, many find their habits and personality traits harder to change. Thirty-one-year-old Richard confesses: “I've spent a decade on self-improvement and the habits that I nailed down when I was in my early 20's are far more enduring and stable than I am working on now”.[6] Richard goes further to state: "I certainly feel that as time passes, you settle into routines which are much harder to change. Part of that is because life becomes busier as I get older, but also my brain seems fixed".[7] Carol Rothwell, an occupational psychologist, lends her voice: “It is true that as we age, we find it more difficult to develop, and some people become more stuck in their ways”.[8]

Rothwell, however, believes that the process is much more complicated than being discussed, as who we are cannot be reduced to mere products of a fixed blueprint or our age. She believes that a combination of experiences, our opportunities, and motivation influences the development of our full potential. Hence, even past thirty, a person continues to fine-tune some areas of his life as experiences unfold and are affected by major life events such as

---

[4] Hosie, 19.05.2020.

[5] Hosie, 19.05.2020.

[6] Hosie, 19.05.2020.

[7] Hosie, 19.05.2020.

[8] Hosie, 19.05.2020.

having children, starting a new job, or suffering bereavement. So, rather than talking of our personalities as being plastered by age thirty, she preferred to talk of them as being half plastered, as some change can still happen.[9] For American psychologist Paul T. Costa Jr., "It's not that personality is fixed and can't change. But it is [only] relatively stable and consistent, so that further personality change, and invariably habitual change, require some extra effort.[10] The long and short of these psychologists' theorics is that, although we do not simply become static monsters as we grow older,[11] the ability to change can be a little difficult.

The implication is that the period for acquiring habits, good or bad, is not eternally elastic. There comes a time when the elasticity of growth is exhausted. Consequently, taking in new habits becomes a much more difficult task. Bad attitudes become much more difficult to drop, just as good attitudes become difficult to take in. At that time, for instance, it becomes very difficult and even quite unlikely for a dishonest or greedy person to drop those vices. Conversely, it becomes very difficult and quite unlikely for an honest or generous person to abandon these good attitudes.

Flor McCarthy presents Dostoevsky's frightening explanation that "The second half of a person's life is usually made up of the habits acquired during the person's first half of life.[12] The older one

---

[9] Hosie, 19.05.2020.

[10] Hosie,19.05.2020.

[11] Kathryn Kattalia, "Our Personalities Stop Changing Once We Turn 30, Science Says, But It's Not As Depressing As It Sounds." https://www.bustle.com.

[12] McCarthy, Year C, 307.

gets, the more difficult it becomes to adjust certain habits. So, at an older age, behavioural change can be much more difficult and require more effort. It is therefore important for young people to put in more effort in the struggle to attain self-mastery in the first phase of human growth, as it becomes more difficult at a later age. Scripture says: "If you gathered nothing in your youth, how can you find something in your old age?" (Prov. 22:6).

The point must be made here that the journey towards self-mastery is not entirely and exclusively a human endeavour. The journey involves God. Therefore, it is never too late to embark on this journey. Moreover, at an advanced age, a person is supposed to have the advantage of the wisdom that comes with age. The older a person is, the more experienced and mature they are in dealing with life issues.

Chapter 29

OCCASIONS OF ERROR

"Do not be deceived: Bad company ruins good morals." (1 Cor. 15:33)

Authentic human development and the attainment of self-mastery are impossible if one does not get one's values right. One of the factors that can hinder a person from getting their values right is error. Every error made constitutes a setback on the journey towards self-mastery. Therefore, the person on the journey towards self-mastery must make concerted efforts to avoid occasions of error. Error means to be wrong.[1] An error is something done wrong. It could be a mistake or an inaccuracy.[2] An error presupposes a wrong choice from options among which one of the options is right. When a person chooses an option other than the correct one, they are said to have committed an error. In this sense, an error can be referred to as "a bad decision".[3]

To commit an error is to stray from what is right, and to stray from what is right is to stray from the truth. It means to deviate from what is good or best in the circumstances. It can occur due to poor judgement, lowering the standards of judgement. An error is a deviation from correctness, accuracy, or truth. It could also mean

[1] *The Oxford Minireference Dictionary (New).* Oxford: Oxford, 1995.

[2] *Oxford Advanced Lerner's Dictionary (Fourth Edition).* Oxford: Oxford, 1993.

[3] *Macmillan English Dictionary (Second Edition).* Oxford: Macmillan, 2007.

believing that which seems right but is not.[4] An error takes a person off track, and the person can only get back on track by aligning. Errors provide an opportunity for learning for the wise.

Although an error can cause serious damage, not every error may necessarily constitute evil. As long as an error is committed unintentionally, it does not constitute wrongdoing. Such may have occurred due to a misjudgement. A misjudgement could result from many factors, such as a person's disposition, ignorance, fear and violence, confusion, bias, stress, overconfidence, wrong advice, etc. In this case, the error involves a mental judgement by which a person holds something false to be true or something true to be false.[5] An error of judgement can lead to an error of decision and an error of decision can lead to an error of action. A decision made in error often leads to a bad action.

The culpability of an error is determined only by whether the error was avoidable or not avoidable in the circumstances. The intention, options, and time available for the decision and execution of the action are all taken into consideration. An error committed out of carelessness amounts to negligence. Issues of liability arise when a person who commits an error vehemently refuses to admit it when confronted with the truth. At this point, he incurs liability for their actions. Repeated commission of the same error despite corrections may be a strong suggestion that the person has a very low level of self-mastery or none at all. Such a person is liable.

---

[4] *The New International Webster's Comprehensive Dictionary of English Language (Encyclopedic Edition).* Naples: Trident, 2004.

[5] https://www.newadvent.org.

Christian moral thought has always emphasised the avoidance of occasions for sin. According to Thomas Pazhayampallil, an occasion to sin is "an external circumstance which implies an impulse or allurement to sin with a consequent likelihood or danger of sinning".[6] Avoiding occasions to sin is a strategy against temptation.[7] By avoiding occasions to sin, one gets rid of any external circumstances that can serve as objects or pave the way for sin. Circumstances to sin are external; they are things that one does not have the power to control. Avoidance of occasions to sin must not be used as a pretext to escape confronting thoughts[8] or develop hatred towards people whose way of life we may not agree with.

John Hardon, in Modern Catholic Dictionary, defines occasion to sin as: "Any person, place, or thing that of its nature or because of human frailty can lead one to do wrong, thereby sinning. If the danger is certain and probable, the occasion is proximate; if the danger is slight, the occasion becomes remote".[9] An occasion to sin is a situation that makes it easier for one to sin.[10]

Drawing from the concept of avoiding occasions to sin, we can also talk of the avoidance of occasions of error. From the records of history, there is only one person who never committed an error, and that is Jesus of Nazareth (1 Peter 1:19; 2:22; Heb. 4:15; 7:26).

---

[6] Thomas Pazhayampallil, *Pastoral Guide, Vol. 1.* Bangalore: Kristu Jyoti, 2004. p. 331.

[7] Karl-Heinz Peschke, *Christian Ethics: Moral Theology in the Light of Vatican I, Vol. 1.* Bangalore: Theological, 1996). p. 312.

[8] Karl, 131.

[9] John Hardon, *Modern Catholic Dictionary.* https//therealpresence.org/archives/Q_and_A/Q_and_A_024.htm.

[10] John Bartunek, https://catholicexchange.com/occasion-sin-sin.

The same Christ offers us grace, through the Holy Spirit, in our struggle against error and sin. Although human, Christians can minimise committing errors as much as possible to the barest minimum. What the Christian needs is due diligence in applying decision-making principles.

The emphasis needs to be on the point that errors often cause harm, sometimes grievous harm, to individuals, others, or both. Therefore, it is incumbent on each Christian to do all that is within their strength to avoid falling into error. To avoid error, a Christian must not exclude God from the equation. Every decision made by the Christian must be predicated on a Christian principle. Jesus summarises these principles in the golden rule: "Do to others as you would have them do to you" (Luke 6:31; Matt. 7:12). This golden rule implies sensitivity. Hundreds of years before Jesus Christ, some deep thinkers held similar principles. For instance, Confucius, who lived between 552 and 479 BC, stated, "What you do not wish upon yourself, extend not to others."[11]. Epicurus, who lived around 350 BC, similarly held, "Neither do harm nor be harmed."[12]. Christians always need to consider the effect of their decisions on themselves first.

Keeping God in the decision-making equation means that decisions are weighed on the scale of the Word of God to determine their acceptability. Very important also, Christians need to avoid settling for mediocrity. Moreover, every effort should be made to gather as much information as possible for the decision-making process. The motive of one's decision, as well as the general good of

[11] https://www.invaji.com/confucius-quotes/.

[12] *Internet Encyclopedia of Philosophy*.https://iep.utm.edu/epicur/.

the effect of that decision on one's community, needs to be borne in mind. Whether the decision will jeopardise one's integrity is another consideration.[13] In all of these, one must pray for and allow God's wisdom and objectivity to guide one's decision-making.

One thing that can never be underrated is the possibility of influence in the commission of errors. While confidants, relations, friends, and guides can sometimes be valuable assets at crucial moments of decision-making, caution is warranted. Some can lead one to commit errors. Hence, each person needs to choose their confidants carefully to ensure that their value orientations are not in sync. There could be confidants whose admonition could be parochial and from personal feelings, sentiments, or opinions not predicated on God's wisdom and objectivity. Job's friends: Eliphaz, Bildad, and Zophar are examples. Although they shared in Job's pains in his moment of trial, their counsels were quite inconsistent with Job's faith (Job 2:11-30). It is good to be watchful because some counselors are after their own interest (Sirach 37:7). One's counselors should be only those who fear God and keep his commandments (Sirach 37:12). In the same vein, one is to seek to understand God's Word itself from authentic interpreters who have been properly trained for the job. This is necessary because there is much misinformation, even from certain preachers today, which can lead people into error.

Our behaviours are products of our thoughts. Positive thoughts manifest in positive behaviours just as negative thoughts manifest in negative behaviours. Positive behaviours both lead to and are

---

[13] https://www.watermark.org/blog/decision-making-principples.

signs of self-mastery. Similarly, negative behaviours both lead to and manifest a low level of, or absence of, self-mastery. Therefore, the journey towards self-mastery requires ensuring that one's mind is fed with the right ideas. Whatever the mind is fed with is as important as what one's body is fed with. Ideas from friends, the people we talk with, the books we read, the films we watch, the music we listen to, all form part of our mental diet. They all influence us positively or negatively in our struggle to attain self-mastery. Consequently, the mind needs a balanced mental diet, just as the body needs a balanced diet. A balanced mental diet keeps the mind healthy and produces good behaviours, just as a balanced diet of food keeps the body healthy and helps it function efficiently, with minimal or rare chances of error.

Holy Scriptures counsel us to listen to and accept only wise advice to gain wisdom (Prov. 19:20). They also teach that whoever walks with the wise becomes wise. Anyone who walks with fools suffers harm (13:20). St. Paul expresses the fear that bad company can lead to an exchange of ideas that can lead to error and even the possibility of ruining good morals (1 Cor. 15:33). The company could be human company or some other thing. In metaphoric language, Jesus speaks about the removal of any part that causes one to sin (Mt 5:29-30). Therefore, everyone has a duty to do everything humanly possible to avoid falling into error. Even though not every error constitutes a sin, it is nonetheless not good for a person on the journey towards self-mastery. Repeated commission of errors is antithetical to the journey towards self-mastery because it is a big hindrance.

Chapter 30

CURING ERRORS

"I will get up and go to my Father and say to him, 'Father, I have sinned against heaven and before you." (Luke 15:18)

We have seen that the journey towards self-mastery requires concerted effort to avoid opportunities to make mistakes. Despite all efforts, one may, due to wounded human nature, ignorance, and misinformation, fall into error at one time or another. When that happens, the only way out is to make haste to cure the error. The Holy Bible calls on defaulters to correct their errors by retracing their steps and making amends. Having returned to his senses, the prodigal son realised his error and decided to seek a cure by going back to his father to ask for forgiveness. Peter told the Israelites to repent and turn to God for their sins to be forgiven (Acts 3:19). Jesus teaches that if a person realises that his brother has something against him while in an offertory procession, he is not to proceed with the offering. The person is to keep it around the altar, go back, make peace, and then return to make the offering (Matt. 5:23-24).

The curing of errors entails serious efforts to make amends and to return to the path of the struggle towards self-mastery. Some stages are involved in this effort. The first stage is to acknowledge the error. This is possible in a dialogue within one's inner self. The purpose of doing this is not to evoke guilt and dwell on it. It is meant to serve as a springboard to the next stage in addressing the error committed. However, some fear facing their mistakes. They dread being alone in the quietness of their inner selves.[1] Facing their mistakes exposes their weaknesses, bangs their ego, and makes them feel bad and defeated. Hence, some would rather deny their errors and argue in their defence than admit them. They don't want to feel bad or defeated. In fact, however, as long as the person holds on to the error, it means the error holds him down with no hope of cure, and that is the worst defeat. It is like a blind man who insists he can see. How can he be healed? (cf. John 9:42).

The second stage is self-reprimand. This stage requires great courage because self-caution is not easy. Self-reprimand goes hand in hand with the resolve to make concerted efforts not to commit such an error again. For this resolve to be authentic, it requires a strong commitment by the person not to repeat the same error. This resolution is necessary. The third stage is reconciliation. The person is to reconcile with God and seek his leniency for having disappointed him. Through this reconciliation, the person reconciles himself or herself to himself or herself because they hurt themself each time they commit an error. In cases where the error affected another person or others and caused them pain, the person is to try to reconcile with them. Humility is required at this stage. It works on two fronts. The individual accepts their own imperfection through humility. And humility softens the heart of the person who is offended.

---

[1] Marla Estes, "Aloneness and Inner Peace". https://ashlandtidings.com.

A fourth stage is the setting of a guardrail.[2] A guardrail guards against danger. It is a barrier placed along the edge of a highway or street at dangerous points.[3] to stop a vehicle from rolling into a dangerous spot. Each person has certain areas of their life where they are prone to making mistakes. A trusted friend could serve as a guardrail, alerting a person whenever they see them slipping towards the prone area. In addition, an individual should set boundaries that make it impossible to make the error. This state also requires a resolve to seek the right information to prevent errors associated with misinformation.

The fifth stage is restitution. The person to whom one's error has caused harm or damage deserves compensation. Suppose you have the capacity to make restitution without anyone demanding it. This helps heal the hurt you caused the person you hurt. In the sixth stage, one needs to seek grace from God for a true cure and the ability to stay off the window of error. Without the help of God, no one can succeed in keeping their resolve, and the struggle to attain self-mastery will be a vain endeavour.

---

[2] https://www.biblestudytools.com/blogs/chris-russell/how-to-fix-bad-decisions.html.

[3] *Merriam-Webster Dictionary* (since 1828).

Chapter 31

DELAY YOUR CONCLUSIONS

"Do not find fault before you investigate; examine first, and then criticise".

(Sirach 11:7)

A lovely little girl held two apples in both hands. Her mother came in and softly requested with a smile, "Sweetheart, could you please give your mum one of your apples? The girl looked up at her mum for a few seconds, then suddenly took a quick bite of one apple, then the other. The mum felt the smile on her face freeze. Disappointing thoughts of mothering a little greedy girl enveloped her mind. She felt so bad that she had added a greedy creature to the stream of greedy people on earth. She, however, tried hard not to reveal her disappointment and waited a little to see the end. Finally, the little girl handed one of the bitten apples to her mum and said, "Mummy, here you are." This is the sweeter one.

Thank God the mother did not conclude but waited to the end. The little angel was trying to taste the two apples to make sure she gave her mother the sweeter one. The interpretation of an action needs to consider three factors: the object, the intention, and the circumstances[1]. These factors are necessary for evaluating the rightness or wrongness of an action. A conclusion drawn without evaluating the action against these factors risks error. Therefore, there is always the need to wait until one has as many facts as possible before concluding. There is, nonetheless, an exception to this

---

[1] CCC, no. 1750.

rule. It does not apply to actions that are intrinsically either good or bad because the object, intention, and circumstances of an action cannot change them from good to bad or vice versa.[2]

When a person concludes without waiting for the facts, they have made a rash judgment. A rash judgement is a firm mental assenting, without sufficient reason, to the existence of a moral defect in another person's words or conduct. Rash judgement is a grave sin against justice.[3] According to the Catechism of the Catholic Church, a person is guilty of rash judgement if he "Even tacitly assumes as true, without sufficient foundation, the moral fault of a neighbour".[4] Sufficient foundation refers to sufficient facts or sufficient information about the neighbour's action or utterances. Peschke defines it as a situation in which another person is judged guilty of wrongdoing without a valid reason.[5] Pazhayampallil refers to it as a conjecture where a wrongdoing is attributed to someone without sufficient evidence. One can avoid rash judgement by ensuring that one interprets one's neighbour's actions or words correctly. Where it is not clear, let the person seek clearance from the one who acted.

One falls into the danger of rash judgement by merely drawing conclusions based on purely logical hypotheses rather than on facts. Such logical hypotheses are presumptions, assumptions, and conjectures, purely an intellectual activity. Any conclusions drawn

---

[2] CCC, no. 1753.

[3] Heribert Jone, *Moral Theology*. Rockfield: Tan, 1993, no. 379.

[4] CCC, no. 2477.

[5] Karl-Heinz Peschke, *Christian Ethics: Moral Theology in the Light of Vatican II, Vol. II*. Bangalore: Theological, 1996, p.346.

based solely on such hypotheses in the evaluation of human conduct are guesswork and hence may not correspond to the facts. Any conclusion drawn on another person's conduct based on such assumptions constitutes a grave violation of justice.

Undeniably, one can arrive at a logically sound conclusion drawing from available premises. However, the conclusion may be invalid if it does not align with the facts. In the evaluation of an action, the validity of the conclusion is determined by the facts rather than intellectual technicalities. A reliance on intellectual technicalities leads to a merely conjectural conclusion, which only the facts can prove right or wrong. Holding onto conjectures as the primary basis for conclusions on a human action is what rash judgement is.

Agreeably, no human being is infallible. Our conclusions about people can sometimes be erroneous, no matter how knowledgeable we are. This is why, after we sometimes rush to conclude and act towards people on serious issues, we later discover that we acted in error. And such an error would have been avoided if only we had delayed our conclusion. Sadly, some of these erroneous decisions and actions of ours would have caused large-scale or near-irreparable damage to a person.

The story of Susanna in Daniel 13 offers a good example. The people and the judges rushed to a conclusion and declared Susanna guilty of the charge brought against her by the elders. However, the elders were the ones who lusted after her. But since she refused, they decided to frame her up. They told the judges and the people that they saw a young man who came to commit adultery with her in the garden. Since they were elders, the people and the judges believed the testimonies and unanimously concluded that she was guilty and decided to condemn her to death (v. 41). It took the wisdom and courage of Daniel, who decided to check on the facts. He demanded that the two elders be kept separate for questioning. He asked each of them to say under which tree two of them were hiding when they saw her committing adultery with the young man. One of the elders said they were under "a mastic tree". The second one said they were under "an evergreen oak". With these facts, Daniel exposed the two elders' lies and saved the innocent Susanna. This brings out the need for due diligence before concluding, as Sirach rebukes: "There is a rebuke that is untimely" (Sirach 20:1).

No matter your status, no matter how experienced and how knowledgeable you may be, always delay your conclusions until you have the facts. Always give people the opportunity to explain themselves. The only time one may not withhold conclusions even when things aren't that clear is in matters of life and death. This is the only exception to this principle. The Igbo underscore this principle in the proverb: "Ife danu na ani, egbuo ya ozigbo bu agwo," meaning, what falls on the ground from a tree and is killed immediately is a snake".[6] The delay in reaching conclusions is also necessary in view of the fact that certain actions do not have a single, straightjacketed meaning. Some of them have more than one meaning or implication. A rush to a conclusion in such circumstances would mean that one has settled for one of the meanings which the person in question may not have intended. The person in question must be allowed to explain himself to clarify matters.

---

[6] Ignatius Obinwa. Igbo Proverb. 05.02.2020.

Some think that it is a sign of intelligence to conclude hastily, especially in matters that need to be left to wait and for which clarification is needed. It may be and may appear fanciful. But it could actually largely be a sign of impatience and lack of humility. It means the person cannot wait until he has verified the authentic meaning of an action or utterance from the person in question. This is more dangerous for people in positions of leadership because it could lead to rash judgment and unjust sanctions. When the true picture of things is discovered, the leader realises he has committed a blunder and that the harm caused by the sanction cannot be undone. Hence, the need to delay conclusions is necessary.

Another reason conclusions need to be delayed is when dealing with people whose level of education and experience differs from yours. Such people, for want of language, may use certain words that only a careful interrogation and demand for explanation can make them throw more light. Culture is also a factor. Certain actions and utterances in one culture may mean something slightly or even entirely different in another culture. Hence, when it is unclear, it is best to wait patiently and seek clarification before concluding.

The act of holding back one's conclusion until one is sure is not an act of weakness or a sign of being a dullard. It is rather an act of strength, a strong indication of self-mastery. By this, the person waits for the facts on the issues before concluding. Any conclusion reached based on the facts is usually error-free because facts are sacrosanct. The journey to self-mastery requires that one delay one's conclusions as long as one does not have the facts on the matter, to avoid the risk of making innocent people suffer unjustly. Courts use this principle. As a principle, a Court is never to conclude until it has enough facts on a matter and beyond a reasonable doubt. Wise people use this principle too in the functioning of "the courts of their minds".

The story of King Solomon and the two women in 1 Kings 3:16-28 comes to mind. Each of the women insisted on laying claim to the living boy. It was difficult to determine who the real mother was. King Solomon used his God-given wisdom and ordered that the boy be cut into two so that each of them would be given half of the dead boy. Compassion burned in the heart of the real mother for her son. So, she told the King to give the boy to the other woman instead of killing him; "Please, my lord, give her the living boy; certainly, do not kill him" (v. 26). But the other woman was happy that the child was going to be killed so that neither of them would have him. She said, "It [the boy] shall be neither mine nor yours; divide it [the boy]" (v. 27). The responses from the two women revealed the facts, namely, that the real mother would naturally prefer to have her child alive in the hands of another woman rather than have him killed. King Solomon concluded that she was the real mother and ordered the child to be given to her.

The need to delay conclusions until one has the facts is crucial in decision-making. This is even more crucial for those in leadership positions at all levels. It is a needless gamble for a leader to rush to a conclusion on a matter without having the facts at hand. Such a gamble will have serious consequences should the facts come to light, and the leader's conclusion and decision be found to have been reached in error. It automatically punctures the leader's integrity. Such a leader risks being seen by his subjects as unfair, unjust, and victimising. The leader may apologise to cushion the effect, but the harm would have been done, and both the leader and his victim have the scars to live with for life. It is therefore safer to delay the conclusion until the facts are clear and one can make a sound, dependable, and indisputable decision. As a rule, it is better to let the guilty one get away with an offense than to conclude that an innocent person is punished.

Another thing to be wary of is the drawing of conclusions based on suspicion. This is like intellectual deception. But they are different. Intellectual deception is strictly a tendency for intellectuals. Suspicion is both for intellectuals and non-intellectuals. Agreeably, some little suspicion is needed for a healthy and safe life. However, it does not form solid grounds for drawing a sound conclusion. Suspicion can, at best, help one become cautious to avoid the future occurrence of the same thing. It is a very dangerous game to draw a conclusion and go ahead and make an impactful decision, especially a negative one, based on mere suspicion, no matter how reasonable it may be. Reasonable suspicion can only form grounds for the commencement of a discrete investigation into a matter with the aim of establishing the facts. The facts may prove the suspicion right or wrong. Therefore, no matter how strong and reasonable the suspicion may be, once there are no facts, there is no need to conclude.

There is also the temptation to draw conclusions based on intuition. Some people have a vivid imagination. Therefore, based on feelings rather than facts, such deep imaginations can lead them to form an opinion and conclude on what they think is the truth. Intuition is not real and cannot be equated with facts on which to base one's conclusion. Intuition is "An ability to know or understand something through your feelings, rather than by considering facts or evidence".[7] Intuition is a strong voice that speaks within a person, even when the person has no physical proof.[8] Some refer to it as the sixth sense.[9] It means the power to understand a thing, a situation, or somebody's feelings immediately, without facts.[10] Conclusions based on intuition have often largely turned out to be wrong.[11] Sometimes, the intuition is 'spiritualised', and this is a very dangerous dimension because, in such a situation, a person gives his intuition spiritual backing.

The act of delaying conclusions often requires patience. One may not need to be in haste depending on the nature of the matter at stake. Some issues can be very difficult to unravel, making it hard to get to the facts. There is no need to rush. A change in strategy may be needed at some point. Patience enables one to maintain the serenity of mind needed for clear investigation. Impatience puts one under undue pressure, and there is every possibility of being unclear when conducting discreet investigations that lead to the unveiling of facts. And this is not good in the struggle to attain self-mastery.

---

[7] *Macmillan English Dictionary for Advanced Learners, New Edition.* Oxford: Macmillan. P. 2007.

[8] https://www.womenontop.com.

[9] https://www.webmd.com.

[10] *Oxford Advanced Learner's Dictionary, Fourth Edition.* Oxford: Oxford, 1993.

[11] https://www.psychologytoday.com.

Chapter 32

TWO VOICES WITHIN

"And heed the counsel of your own heart,
for no one is more faithful to you than it is." (Sirach 37:13)

One of my most exciting days in primary school was when our Christian Religious Knowledge teacher, Mr. Anthony Ādang, taught us about two faint voices within the heart of each person: the voice of good and the voice of evil. Mr. Ādang explained that each of these faint voices usually urges a person to its bidding. The voice of good cries out within, urging the person to do the right thing, while the voice of evil urges the person to do the wrong thing. Mr. Ādang told us then that the good voice is the voice of the person's guardian angel, while the bad voice is that of the devil. As children, he told each of us always to obey the voice of our guardian angel and discard the voice of the devil. This took place around 1982 in our primary four, when we were nine.

That particular class was very real to me, and it left a mark that the memories of it have remained ever fresh in my mind. It was particularly interesting to me to realise that God wonderfully made me with a guide within me, which I only needed to recognise and choose to act as it directed me. Much later in life, I came to discover that this faint voice Mr. Ādang referred to as the guardian angel's voice in each of us is the voice of conscience. In that lesson, he achieved two things: he awakened the consciousness of conscience in each of us and the power within us to make our own decisions and take ownership of them at that early age.

God endowed each of us with this unique voice.[1] This voice cries out within and is heard by every conscientious person. It analyses every action before us, to determine its rightness and/or wrongness, and gives assent or dissent. According to the Catechism of the Catholic Church, this voice is located deep down in the innermost part of each person's heart.[2] There, each person is alone with God, who is the truth (John 14:6). This strategic location makes it impossible for any external interference. Adimonye calls this voice within 'a guiding light'.[3] Conscience is the rational faculty in each of us that searches for objective truth in the Scriptures, the revealed Word of God, either directly or relationally, in the teachings of the Church, and in other norms of right reason.

There is an interesting interaction between God and the individual in his conscience. At first, God speaks to the individual right deep inside his conscience. God then, without interference, allows the individual to make his choice. At this level, God then stands as a witness.[4] The reason for God's non-interference is the tremendous respect he has for the individual's freedom, which is his excellent gift to humanity (Gen 2:16-17). Freedom allows the individual's heart the latitude to navigate towards good.[5] By this same free-

---

[1] CCC, no. 1776; LG, 16.

[2] CCC, no. 1776.

[3] Adimonye, Aloysius M. *My Conscience: My Guiding Light.* Enugu: SNAAP, 2002.

[4] LG, 16.

[5] LG, 17.

dom, however, man sometimes chooses to act contrary to God's voice. Hence, it is by this same freedom that each person shall be held accountable for his choices.

The voice of conscience is understood to operate before an action is carried out (antecedent), as the action is being carried out (concomitant), or after the action has been carried out (consequent).[6] Conscience, therefore, never ceases to function either before an action is carried out or as it is being carried out or after it has been carried out. And at any point, one realises that one has made the wrong choice, and one is expected to make a U-turn in favor of the right choice. The voice of conscience is genuine and always leads one to the right choices. By means of it, one assumes responsibility for one's actions.[7]

Noteworthy is that this voice within is a subjective human faculty, with its limitations and thus subject to error. But the errors can be minimised by adhering to the moral principle of doing good at all times and shunning evil. This principle does not allow one to do evil so that good may come out of it. Moreover, one is to be consistent in doing to others only that which one wants done to one (Mt 7:2; Lk 6:31).[8] This brings to the fore the necessity of the proper formation of conscience with the proper education with the Word of God and the teachings of the Church, to enable it to conform to objective truth as; "A well-formed conscience is upright and truthful. It formulates its judgments according to reason, in

---

[6] Karl-Heinz Peschke, *Christian Ethics: Moral Theology in the Light of Vatican II, Vol. 1*. Bangalore: Theological, 1996, p. 174.

[7] CCC, no. 1781.

[8] CCC, no. 1789.

conformity with the true good that is willed by the wisdom of the creator".[9]

All said and done, no one should neglect the place of the voice within him in the struggle to attain self-mastery. Sirach admonishes each person: "And heed the counsel of your own heart, for no one is more faithful to you than it is" (37:13). Hence, everyone has the obligation to listen to and follow the dictates of his well-formed conscience. As a matter of fact, no external authority should interfere or force one to act against or contrary to the dictates of his voice within.[10] The Catechism of the Catholic Church particularly points out that man has the right to personally make his decisions in conscience and in freedom without meddling: "He must not be forced to act contrary to his conscience. Nor must he be prevented from acting according to his conscience, especially in religious matters".[11] This freedom, however, comes with responsibility and does not indulge in blame-shifting as our first parents did (Gen. 3:12-13).

The autonomy of conscience does not preclude consultations on certain issues that may arise. It is a way of seeking education to clear up doubts about the issues so that one can make one's decision from an informed point of view. In the final analysis, the individual has to make their decision. One who listens to one's conscience always acts according to truth, which is the foundation of virtue and hence the key in the struggle to attain self-mastery.

---

[9] CCC, no. 1783.

[10] McBrien, Richard. *Catholicism*. London: St. Pauls, 2008. p. 972.

[11] CCC, no. 1782.

Chapter 33

GRACE CRYING FOR COOPERATION

'But he said to me, My grace is sufficient for you....' (2 Cor. 12:9)

It would be unrealistic for anyone to pretend that the struggle to attain self-mastery is easy. It is tough because we are swimming against the odds of our wounded nature, stemming from original sin called concupiscence. Concupiscence is the propensity of human nature to sin due to the wound of original sin, which weakened man's original nature.[1] Concupiscence is the temporal consequence in the baptised such as suffering, illness, physical death, frailties inherent in life in forms of weaknesses of character and the inclination to sin.[2] They do not go after baptism. This is what St. James identifies as the desires that tempt us (James 1:14). Concupiscence remains after baptism, so that, relying on the grace given by Christ, the baptised can prove himself in the struggle of his Christian life.[3] Jesus himself warns that the sinful thoughts that lead us to sin are not from without but from within the heart (Matt. 15:19).

---

[1] John A. Hardon, *Pocket Catholic Dictionary*. New York: DOUBLEDAY, 1985. p. 86.

[2] CCC, no. 1264.

[3] CCC, no. 1426.

St. Thomas Aquinas refers to concupiscence as "...a strong appetite [desire] arising in the sensitive part of man".[4] St. Augustine describes concupiscence as the human person's spontaneous desire for material or sensual satisfaction, and as an effect of original sin.[5] Another name for concupiscence is passion, referring to any form of intense desire. Christian theology sees it as a movement of man's sensitive appetites against his reason.[6] It is the soul's passionate movement towards whatever is perceived to be desirable. Concupiscence can be so forceful that it exerts strong pressure on the human will at the moment of decision-making. It can sway a person's decision-making by weakening the intellect.[7] It, however, does not vindicate one from liability for one's actions.

Concupiscence is left for us to wrestle with as a consequence of original sin. Hence, no one can make meaningful progress on the journey towards perfection and self-mastery on their own. We need the grace of God, which God himself has promised us in sufficient supply in our struggle to conquer our weaknesses and untamed excesses that manifest in aberrant behaviour (2 Cor. 12:9). Although concupiscence is forceful and capable of exerting a very strong influence on the human will, it does not incapacitate the will's ability to make its decisions. All that we need to do is to cooperate with the grace of God by refusing to consent to our ungod-

---

[4] Paul J. Glenn, *A Tour of the Summa of St. Thomas Aquinas.* Bangalore: Theological, 2007. p. 124.

[5] Richard McBrien, *Catholicism.* Ibadan: St. Paul's, 2008. p. 187.

[6] Thomas Pazhayampallil, *Pastoral Guide, Vol.1.* Bangalore: Kristu Jyoti, 2004. p. 85.

[7] Richard P. McBrien (Ed), *The HarperCollins Encyclopedia of Catholicism.* New York: HarperCollins, 1995. p. 343-4.

ly desires, to resist them by the grace of Christ who gives us strength (Phil. 4:13).

This underscores the necessity of remaining connected with Jesus, the vine, to continuously draw strength from him.[8] to assist us in the struggle to attain self-mastery. Jesus made it very categorical: "For apart from me, you can do nothing" (John 15:5). This expresses the need for the follower of Christ to maintain an inseparable relationship with him. Grace flows from this connection and helps the Christian to make progress in the struggle to attain self-mastery. Grace attracts God's merits, which help the Christian to abound in good works.[9] A life of grace assists the follower of Christ in building character and gives him delight in doing good.[10] It will be impossible for a Christian to maintain any moral balance without grace.[11] Heartwarming is the assurance that God's grace is never in short supply. St. Paul states it boldly: "But he said to me, 'My grace is sufficient for you, for my power is made perfect in weakness'" (2 Cor. 12:9).

---

[8] *The International Bible Commentary*. Bangalore: Theological, 1998. p. 1563.

[9] CCC, no. 2011.

[10] CCC, no. 1810.

[11] CCC, no. 1811.

Chapter 34

WEAK BUT NOT WRECKED

"All have sinned and fall short of the glory of God." (Rom. 3:23)

No human being was born a champion. It is determination and persistence in actualising their talents that make them champions. I watched a short video of an adventurous little boy attempting to jump on his small rubber stool. He tried several times but fell back, never giving up. He kept trying day after day until one day, he finally succeeded. He clapped for himself as he stood on top of the small rubber stool filled with excitement. The little boy did not allow himself to be encumbered by the impediments of his size and strength. He never gave up after trying several times and failing until he achieved his aim. What kept him on were determination and persistence.

Determination and persistence are two qualities that characterise the journey of any champion. This is the case with many great sportsmen and women. Each of them has a targeted level of proficiency he seeks to attain and never rests in his struggle until he reaches his goal. Their coaches play a vital role in the struggle. The coach never consoles the trainee by pointing out his limitations. He focuses more on the trainee's capabilities. He pushes the trainee on and makes him feel he can achieve his target. He challenges the trainee's fighter spirit, evokes willpower, and keeps him determined and focused. In the final analysis, most trainees can surmount their limitations and emerge as champions. These same attitudes of determination and persistence also play out in business. In the struggle to attain self-mastery, the two attitudes of determination and persistence are equally indispensable.

In the context of this discussion, determination means a firm and definitive resolve or decision to do something.[1] Persistence means to endure without giving up on a course.[2] Another word for persistence is perseverance. The attainment of self-mastery is a journey and a struggle that an individual must undertake with determination and persistence. This is because the person is struggling to surmount human limitations due to the weaknesses and untamed excesses of our human nature, which result from the injury of original sin. The words of St. Paul, "All have sinned and fall short of the glory of God", are perhaps the best expression of the reality of our injured human nature.

God made us very good (Gen. 1:31). He made man only a little less than God and crowned him with glory and honour (Psalm 8:5). But original sin dealt a blow to humanity (Gen. 3), making us fall short of God's glory. However, the wound of original sin did not wreck humanity. It only incurred a weakness in humanity, leaving lasting consequences on all of humanity, whereby all became implicated (CCC 402). The sin did not wreck humanity. It only brought a deprivation to humanity's original holiness and justice. In other words, human nature was not totally corrupted but only wounded in the natural powers proper to it and thereby made subject to ignorance, suffering, and the dominion of physical

---

[1] *Merriam-Webster Dictionary* (Since 1828).

[2] *Merriam-Webster Dictionary* (Since 1828).

death, and an evil inclination to sin called concupiscence (CCC 405).

The good news is that God did not leave humanity without help. Restoration came when he sent his Son, our Lord Jesus Christ, to die on the cross (Rom 3:24-25). Hence, by baptism, a Christian receives the life of Christ's grace, which erases original sin and turns him back towards God, even though the weakness inflicted on his nature and the inclination to evil persist, thereby summoning him to a spiritual battle (CCC 405). This is the proper context in which our Lord's call to perfection (Mt 5:48) becomes relevant, and this is the proper context for our struggle to attain self-mastery. Our human weakness is not such that it incapacitates us from rising above our fallen state. It did not render us helpless in becoming better beings; it only threw us a challenge. With determination and persistence, we can get there.

Therefore, the Christian struggling to attain self-mastery needs to realise that he is not only weak but not wrecked. We have the charge and ability to regain control over our evil inclinations. What is needed in this struggle is determination and persistence. Although it's a lifelong endeavour, a person can make very reasonable appreciative progress. No doubt, perfection is of God alone (Mark 10:8), but Jesus calls us to strive to be perfect like God. The struggle to attain self-mastery is, therefore, a struggle to become more and more like God. No one can get there a hundred percent (100%), but each can attain a great deal near the target. A person can greatly make gains over his weaknesses and untamed excesses, and so assert himself in the control of his conduct.

The greatest setback, and a very tragic one at that, is when a person makes the fact of human weakness a shelter he runs to, hiding behind it to evade responsibility for his aberrant conduct. By so doing, they make the fact of human weakness a hideout for their effortlessness in putting up a struggle against their weaknesses and untamed excesses. This kind of thinking is defeatist and reflects a poor understanding of human weakness itself. There are inherent limitations on human nature due to original sin, which are largely conquerable with serious struggle.

In this struggle, the kind of determination and persistence of the little boy in the story above is what we need, rather than taking refuge in weakness and giving room for excuses and self-pity. Pastors of souls are the coaches of their members in the struggle towards self-mastery. They are to challenge the positive energy in members, awaken the fighter spirit in them, and spur their will and their capacity for self-conquest. A constant reminder to them that they are weak does grave psychological damage to the fighter spirit in them. It paves the way for a possible relapse into self-pity, a lack of effort, and despondency. It dampens the power of the will in the struggle to be better moral beings.

Statements such as "God understands that we are weak" when one is either not making any effort at all or only very little effort to achieve self-conquest are theologically misleading and morally compromising. God only understands when a person has put in their best but still falls short of their target and God's expectations. Such a person can be said to have put on a good fight like St. Paul (2 Tim. 4:7). This is where God's grace, which is sufficiently available to support the person in the struggle, comes in. In the struggle towards attaining self-mastery, a person must avoid taking refuge in human weakness. He must put in all his effort in the struggle because the struggle is what matters. Jesus exhorts us, "Strive to enter by the narrow door" (Luke 13:24). Let the struggle to attain self-mastery begin and be sustained. It amounts to a moral compromise and mediocrity for a person to settle for a low standard of behaviour manifest in aberrance and below his dignity as a human being under the guise of "that is who I am".

Chapter 35

OIL FOR THE JOURNEY

"If any of you lacks Wisdom,
let him ask God who gives to all men generously." (James 1:5)

Wisdom is a familiar term but scarcely clearly understood by many, and hence difficult to define. Those who have attempted to define it have done so variously, thereby bringing so many things into it. Ordinarily, it is defined as "Experience and knowledge shown in making decisions and judgments; good judgment; advisability; common sense".[1] Also, it is defined as the ability to make good decisions based on knowledge and experience gained over a long period.[2] Elsewhere, wisdom is understood as the power of true and right discernment; a high degree of knowledge; to be wise.[3] According to *The Webster's Unabridged Dictionary,* wisdom is "knowledge, and the capacity to make due use of it".[4]

Christian theology places wisdom in perspective by identifying it as one of the seven gifts of the Holy Spirit, along with understanding, counsel, fortitude, knowledge, piety, and fear of the

---

[1] *Oxford Advanced Learner's Dictionary (Fourth Edition).* Oxford: Oxford University, 1993.

[2] *Macmillan English Dictionary for advanced Learners (New Edition).* Oxford: Macmillan, 2007.

[3] *The International Webster's Comprehensive Dictionary of English Language (Encyclopedic Edition).* Naples: Typhoon International, 2004.

[4] "Defining Spiritual Wisdom for Yourself". https://www.everydayhealth.com.

Lord.[5] These gifts of the Holy Spirit are permanent supernatural dispositions that help sustain the Christian's moral life by making him docile in following the Holy Spirit's promptings.[6] This earns them the qualification and name, as well as spiritual or divine gifts. Wisdom is the application of what one knows to be good in everyday life; "A perfection of the understanding, enabling the just man to judge all things according to divine standards, to take 'God's point of view'".[7] The peculiarity of the Christian understanding of wisdom lies in its contemplation of things according to the mind of God. Wisdom is needed, and it is the oil in the journey towards attaining self-mastery.

In Christian understanding, wisdom and knowledge are closely related but not the same. Hence, wisdom is not to be confused with possession of knowledge, which is acquaintance with facts, truths, and principles. The application of knowledge is what is referred to as wisdom. If knowledge is not applied appropriately, it is the opposite of wisdom.[8] This means that excellence in knowledge or intelligence is not the same as wisdom. One could possess and score a *Summa Cum Laude* in knowledge and yet manifest the opposite of wisdom in one's life. This explains why a mind that possesses wis-

---

[5] CCC, no. 1831.

[6] CCC, no. 1830.

[7] Donald Attwater (Ed.), *A Catholic Dictionary* (Third Edition). Illinois: Tan Books, 1907.

[8] "Defining Spiritual Wisdom for Yourself". https://www.everydayhealth.com.

dom, although less educated, can often make sound judgments far better than a highly educated or skilled mind that lacks wisdom.[9]

Wisdom is needed to translate acquired knowledge and experiences into concrete actions and good choices in life. It is with this understanding that wisdom can be understood as the concrete application of knowledge and experience to the good choices of daily life. Wisdom guides the mind in the application of knowledge according to the mind of God. It navigates the mind towards God, who is truth.

Divine wisdom is generally associated with God as its source (Prov. 2:6). The Holy Bible contains the famous story of the young King Solomon, to whom God offered the choice of any desire. He decided to ask for wisdom. God was impressed by his choice and added many more blessings to him, such as riches, fame, power, and honour (1 Kings 3:5-14). God added all these to him because God knew that, with wisdom, he could manage them effectively.

The Holy Bible sings the praises of wisdom and presents it as a treasure to be desired by all. Those who are wise cherish wisdom while fools despise it (Prov. 1:7). It is a blessing to find wisdom and understanding (3:13). One is not to forsake wisdom (4:6). The possession of wisdom is by far better than the possession of jewels (8:1-12). Wisdom flows from the mouth of the righteous (10:31). Wisdom is much better than gold (16:16). Fear of the Lord is a sign of wisdom (Psalm 111:10). According to Jesus, it is those who have wisdom that understand the secrets of the kingdom of heaven (Matt. 3:11). In the parable of the ten virgins, the who had wisdom

---

[9] Attwater. *A Catholic Dictionary.*

were the ones who went to receive the bridegroom (Matt. 25:1-13). Wisdom that comes from God is pure (James 3:17). Those who heed the teachings of Christ gain wisdom because he is the wisdom of God (1 Cor. 1:30).

A person with knowledge and talent without wisdom could apply them destructively. A person on the journey towards self-mastery needs wisdom to guide their decisions and to apply their knowledge. Choices in the endeavour of conquering one's weaknesses and untamed excesses could be far more complicated than one can ever imagine. Therefore, one needs wisdom always to be rightly guided on the path of struggle. It is the oil that lights up the way for the mind to make the right decisions. Wisdom is the gift needed by the will to overpower and surmount the pressure of the inclinations of our human weaknesses and untamed excesses in the evaluation, choices, and execution of our actions.

Even though the guide of Wisdom is key in the struggle to attain self-mastery, it is a hard and unpopular path. Although reasonable and best, there are times when wisdom's decisions can be very bitter, either for the individual, others, or both. A distinctive characteristic marks decisions guided by wisdom. They are not made for gain but for good. If gain turns out to accompany it, fine. This is not personal good but the good of all, also known as the common good. Decisions guided by wisdom are sometimes not acceptable to all. Only those who are wise understand wise decisions. Nonetheless, wisdom is the surest guide to making the right decisions in life. The journey to the attainment of and the actual living of a life of self-mastery necessarily requires wisdom. It is oil for the journey.

Chapter 36

DO NOT BE OVERWHELMED

"Courage! Do not be afraid, for I am your God; I will strengthen you, I will help you, I will uphold you with my victorious right hand." (Isaiah 41:10).

Feelings of being overwhelmed are not only inimical to the struggle to attain self-mastery but are crippling. To be overwhelmed is to be completely overcome by force or numbers or overpowered by thought or feeling.[1] It means to feel engulfed, swamped, or submerged by something or a situation. Being overwhelmed is feeling overpowered and emotionally crushed.[2] When a person is overwhelmed, it means something has a very strong emotional effect on the person to the extent that they feel temporarily incapacitated or helpless. It can also mean defeating someone or something with a lot of force.[3]

As an experienced Crisis Counsellor, Saysi Winter explains that when people say they are overwhelmed, it can have both positive and negative connotations. In a positive sense, it can mean an ecstatic feeling in response to positive experiences, such as an amazing act of love or kindness, whereby the person feels temporarily stunned and cannot think of a sensible response at the time, until the person has calmed down or taken a break. In the negative sense, it can mean that a person is temporarily unable to think

[1] *Merriam-Webster Dictionary* (soft copy).

[2] Wiktionary (soft copy).

[3] Cambridge Dictionary (soft copy).

clearly due to emotional distress, causing them to experience significant distraction. This can result from negative emotions such as sadness, anger, or frustration.[4] A person can also feel overwhelmed by a combination of both positive and negative experiences.

The negative sense of being overwhelmed is the sense dealt with here. This is the sense in which a person's weaknesses and aberrant tendencies could influence the mind of someone embarking on the journey towards self-mastery. They can stare one in the face, making one feel intimidated, which can lead to feeling overwhelmed. And once this feeling becomes strong and asserts itself in a person's mind, it could, in turn, become a significant source of discouragement. As a matter of fact, even just one such weakness or aberrant tendency can torment a person and give rise to a feeling of being overwhelmed. This was perhaps what David felt in his heart when he confessed, "For I know my transgressions, and my sin is always before me" (Psalm 50:3).

The Holy Bible uses various words and expressions for the reality of being overwhelmed. For example, the Psalmist talks of it as faint-heartedness (61:1-2; 142); Deuteronomy uses fear and dismay (31:8). Through the Prophet Isaiah, God assured his people not to be afraid or dismayed (41:10). Also, in the Bible, being overwhelmed is associated with, and is sometimes synonymous with, fear and anxiety. An example of this is the kind of fear that gripped the disciples in the tumultuous boat while Jesus was asleep. It made them speak to him with a seemingly agitated and desperate expression: "Teacher, do you not care if we perish?" This conveys more

---

[4] Saysi Winter, https://www.quora.com.

than fear; it conveys a feeling of being overwhelmed (Mark 4:35-41). Jesus knew that thoughts of tomorrow's (future) uncertainties can overwhelm his followers. Hence, he admonished them not to be anxious (Matt. 6:34). He promises to give his followers rest from the burdens that overwhelm them (Matt. 11:28).

The journey towards self-mastery is a battle to conquer one's weaknesses and aberrant tendencies. The weaknesses and aberrant tendencies may be many and endemic, and may have eaten very deep, depending on the individual. There is the possibility that upon deciding to embark on the journey towards self-mastery, one becomes fully aware of these many weaknesses and aberrant tendencies, and the extent to which they have taken root. This awareness can lead to feelings of being overwhelmed, resulting in confusion and even discouragement about beginning or continuing the struggle. A person embarking on the journey towards self-mastery needs to be courageous. The person could take on the challenges one after another. In the end, what matters is the courage to begin somewhere and the sustained effort a person puts into the struggle.

Anyone embarking on the struggle towards self-mastery has to be and remain positive and never be overwhelmed. At certain moments, the struggle can get really tough. Whenever this happens, the person needs to put his trust in God with whom everything is possible (Matt. 19:26). He needs to believe in Christ who his disciples; "Courage! Do not be afraid" (Mark 6:49) and who equips his children with the graces to move on (2 Cor. 12:9). The person only needs to put in his best and like the Psalmist, have their eyes looking up to God from whom his help comes (121:1-2).

Chapter 37

KILL EXCUSES

"But they all alike began to make excuses...." (Luke 14:18)

One of the worst enemies one is most surely going to meet in the journey towards self-mastery is the temptation to make excuses. Making excuses involves attempting to lessen blame for one's fault or to provide reasons, explanations, or justifications for the action.[1] According to Chamberlain, making excuses refers to the rationalisations we make in favor of ourselves, others, events, or circumstances. Excuses are reasons we invent to defend a behaviour we have engaged in, to neglect something we are supposed to do, or to negate responsibility.[2]

A person who makes excuses tries to evade responsibility for his actions. Unlike in the case of blaming, where a person plays the innocent victim by shifting the responsibility for his action to another, one who makes excuses primarily intends to vindicate himself by providing reasons to show either that what he has done is not wrong or to evade liability for his action by way of rationalisation. While the main purpose of making excuses is self-vindication, it can sometimes lead to blaming others to vindicate oneself.

There are those to whom the making of excuses has become their stock in trade. There are examples of such people in the Bible.

---

[1] https://languages.oup.com/google-dictionary-en/

[2] Chamberlain H. Guthrie. https://wisdom-trek.com/archive-1/day-116/

A man whom Jesus called gave an excuse to be excused from going to bury his father before returning to follow him (Luke 9:59).

Jesus gave the story of a man who gave a banquet and decided to invite many (Luke 14:16-20). When all was set, the man sent his servants to remind the invitees: "Come for all is now ready". However, all of them failed to turn up and gave excuses. One of them sent the servant back to tell his master that he had bought a new field and was going to see it. Another told the servant to go back and tell his master that he had bought five yokes of oxen and had to go and inspect them. Another one sent the servant to tell his master that he had just married a new wife and could not leave her alone. Besides, he needed to enjoy the warmth of his new wife. And the list of excuses went on and on.

When God sent Gideon to deliver his people from the Midianites, he made an excuse (Judges 6:13-15). King Saul made an excuse to spare some animals, and King Agag did so contrary to God's command (1 Sam. 15:20-21). When God called Jeremiah and sent him, he tried to make an excuse that he was only a youth and did not know how to speak (1:6).

Realising that excuses are serious obstacles to man's response to God's loving invitation, the Psalmist prays for God to keep his heart from being inclined to the making of excuses (141:4). The author of Proverbs admonishes that we should not find excuses to put off things that we need to do. Instead, we are never to rest until we have done what needs to be done (6:4).

Hardly can there be found a person who has never made at least an excuse. We make excuses for things we have done, for things we have failed to do, and for things we do not wish to do.

Unfortunately, the more excuses one makes, the more one stunts the chances of getting things done. This is because a person's excuses gradually become a new reality.[3]

Chamberlain posits that the main reason why people make excuses is fear. Fear of failure, embarrassment, change, uncertainty, responsibility, making mistakes, a perceived lack of confidence, or resources. He further explains that the consequences of making excuses can be very serious and lasting. It prevents one from reaching one's full potential and from recognising one's talents and skills.

On the journey towards self-mastery, making excuses is counterproductive. Instead of facing one's weaknesses and aberrant tendencies, the person makes excuses for them, thereby settling for them as their reality. Anyone, therefore, who wants to make progress on the journey towards self-mastery needs to kill the habit of making excuses.

---

[3] https://medium.com/the-logician/stop-with-the-excuses-its-time-to-make-a-change-87990fc6a9d6 15.07.2021.

Chapter 38

MAKE AN EFFORT

"Why then did you not put my money into the bank, and at my coming, I should have collected it with interest?" (Luke 19:23)

There is one determinant of whether we succeed or fail in life. It is an effort. A person who has succeeded has made an "effort". A person who has failed has made no "effort". Effort means a voluntary exertion of power, a strenuous endeavour,[1] a serious attempt, to try, a conscious exertion of power, or total work done to achieve a particular end.[2] Also, it means an energetic attempt, a struggle, the result of an attempt.[3] It is the physical and mental activity needed to achieve something;[4] a vigorous or determined attempt;[5] an attempt to do something, especially when it involves a lot of hard work.[6] Making an effort is an intentional, deliberate determination to accomplish something.

Jesus tells the story of a nobleman who travelled to a far country and entrusted a pound to each of his ten servants, instructing them to trade with it until his return (Luke 19:12-26). Upon his

---

[1] *The New International Webster's Comprehensive Dictionary of the English Language (Encyclopedic Edition)*. Naples: Typhoon, 2004.

[2] 2021 Merriam-Webster, Inc. 06.02.2021.

[3] *Oxford Advanced Learner's Dictionary of Current English (Fourth Edition)*. Oxford: Oxford, 1993.

[4] https://www.dictionary.cambridge.org.

[5] https://www.lexicon.com.

[6] https://www.ldoceonline.com.

return, he demanded an account of their stewardship. Nine of them traded and made gains. The results for four servants are presented in the story. The first made ten additional pounds, the second made five more, and the third servant made two. Strangely, the fourth servant refused to trade with his pound. He decided to tie it with a napkin and returned it to the nobleman exactly as he had been given. He cited the nobleman's severity as the reason for his failure to trade.

Kodell explains that the parable was originally meant to answer certain germane questions in the early church about when Christ would return and what Christians were supposed to be doing as they awaited his return. The parable made it clear that they were neither to sit idle nor to preserve the *status quo*. They were instead to be meaningfully engaged in bearing witness to him (Acts 1:8), an act expected to bring an increase in the Christian numbers.

In reviewing the servants' stewardship, those who were enterprising were rewarded. But the one who did not trade with his money was not rewarded. Rather, the nobleman ordered that even the unproductive pound in his possession be taken from him and handed over to the one who had more.[7]

One thing stands clear here. The primary basis on which the other servants were rewarded was their effort, not so much because they succeeded in making much gain. Each of them was rewarded with a share in the same kingdom. Conversely, the basis for which the last servant was not rewarded was that he made no effort. Jesus teaches that entering the kingdom is a struggle: "Strive to enter by

---

[7] Jerome Kordell, *The Gospel According to Luke.* Mumbai: St Paul, 2001. p. 94-95.

the narrow door" (Luke 13:24). This means that entering the kingdom of God requires effort.

The nobleman's question: "Why then did you not put my money into the bank, and at my coming I should have collected it with interest?", is purely and simply business sense. If a person, for any reason, cannot trade with money in his possession, the wisest thing to do is to keep it in a bank that will lend it out at interest. And the interest will be shared between the bank and the money's owner. This servant did not do this. He made no effort to add value to the money entrusted to him and did not keep it where it could. Instead, he put it in the path of danger. By just tying it in a napkin and keeping it at home, he exposed the money to theft by domestic deviants or intruders.

The temptation can be very strong to conclude so quickly that many people who fail to make an effort are dumb. This may not always be true, judging from the unproductive servant's smartness. When he heard the nobleman's commentaries on the productive servants and the rewards given them, he knew he was in trouble. He must have sensed that the commentaries on him would be damaging and embarrassing. Therefore, he had to put up a defence to cover his shame smartly. He decided to package a blackmail against the nobleman. His aim must have been to give the nobleman a character dent that would put him in a defensive situation to cripple any possible thoughts of embarrassing him. His calculation was probably to make the nobleman shift his attention to defending his integrity rather than focusing on his failure and running embarrassing commentary on him.

Effort is crucial in all areas of life, but especially in the pursuit of self-mastery. Every human being desires not only to be successful intellectually and materially but also character-wise. Every human being needs to desire to be good because it is good to be good. One-time Vicar General of the Catholic Diocese of Kafanchan, Very Rev. Fr. Ibrahim Bawa Yakubu often says, "It is good to be good and bad to be bad. It is neither bad to be good nor good to be bad".[8]

The desire to be good alone is an act of goodwill. But it does not automatically translate into action, thereby improving the person. The person has to work towards it, and that effort begins. The enemy of success is effortlessness. This is why Anthony Moore opines that the likes of the unenterprising servant cannot even be said to have failed to succeed. In fact, they rarely even reach that stage. They fail before they even get there because they do not even make an effort.[9]

Effort is the starting point in the journey towards self-mastery. It is a significant decision each person must make. Like the king in the parable, God allows us the freedom to decide. God trusts each of us because of the capacity he has put in us. According to Barclay, the king gave his servants money and left each of them to handle it as each thought best. He never interfered.[10] It is in like manner that

---

[8] Very Rev. Fr. Ibrahim Bawa Yakubu. He sent the quote via WhatsApp on 08.02.2021.

[9] Anthony Moore, https://www.medium.com.

[10] William Barclay, *The Daily Study Bible: The Gospel According to Luke.* Bangalore: Theological, 1999. Luke 19:12-26. This is on the parable

God does not interfere with our decisions to grow in virtue and to attain self-mastery, even as he has abundant graces in store for us.

Some get overwhelmed by fear, looking at what is involved in the journey towards self-mastery, and either never get started at all or give up the struggle. Some even consider it an impossibility. Hence, they make no effort. A Christian should not entertain such pessimism because it can lead to losing hope in oneself. Therefore, anyone who has not begun the journey towards self-mastery needs to start now. Some may have begun and failed once or many times. This may have left them feeling devastated and giving up. Effort makes no room for despair. It is said that there are always two best times to start in life. The first is "now" and the second is "now".[11] There is a Chinese proverb which says that, "The best time to plant a tree was twenty years ago. The second-best time is now".[12] So, start now. Make an effort.

---

of the ten-gold money cons. It is St. Luke's version of Matthew's parable of the talents (Mt 25:14-30).

[11] Swandy Banta, Phone conversation 15.01.2021.

[12] Richard H. Smith, https://www.psychologytoday.com. 22.04.2021.

Chapter 39

GIVE IT A GOOD FIGHT

"I have fought the good fight." (2 Tim. 4:7)

At the 1994 Olympics, Nigerian (then Green Eagles) player Rashidi Yekini scored a historic goal that excited fans. Upon hitting the net, the ball lifted high, as if to testify to spectators that the goal was indeed scored. The shot was so strong that it is referred to as Yekini's rocket shot. That shot was not a product of magic but a product of dogged perseverance in practice. Yekini must have exerted all his energy and stamina at the time of kicking that ball. In that shot, Yekini evidently gave his best kick. The struggle to attain self-mastery requires a similar effort.

As he faced the end of his life, St. Paul declared, "I have fought the good fight." This expression is a metaphor for his faithfulness to his calling and for declaring that he had put his best into his mission. St. Paul looks back at the efforts he had put in as a steward of Christ and declares with full confidence, *"I have fought the good fight"*. By this, he declares without doubt that he has put in his best in his struggle to spread the gospel of Christ and in his struggle against evil. This means he put in his best, giving his all in his work. He went all out without reservation.

The Greek word St. Paul uses for fight is *agon.* Athletes use it for a contest in an arena. An athlete uses the word to mean that he has put in his best, after which he either wins or loses. In the use of this word, the athlete's satisfaction is not in whether he wins or not, but in the very fact that he has done his absolute best.[1] According to Ericksen, doing one's best is not about meeting expectations, achievements, or success or failure, but about putting all of one's energy into whatever one sets out to do. St. Paul uses the word *agon* advisedly.

Looking back, at the end of his life, St. Paul knows that he never lived a perfect life. He was a man who struggled with his weaknesses. According to him, the only thing he could boast of was his weaknesses (2 Corr. 11:30; 12:5). He laments his imperfection where he found himself doing those things he hated and not doing those good things he so desired. In fact, he acknowledges that sin lived in him (Rom. 7:13-20). But St. Paul did not give up. He kept struggling with his weaknesses all his life to the best of his ability. This is the source of his satisfaction. And so he can say, "I have fought a good fight."

Barclay cites Barrie, who made the claim at his brother's death: "I can look back, and I cannot see the smallest thing undone".[2] Akiroq Brost says this another way: "Do the best you can. If it doesn't work out, at least you will have the peace of mind knowing you tried."[3] Gift Gaga Mona says, "When you do your best, you become better at what you do".[4] Amos Alonzo Stagg says, "I pray not

[1] William Barclay, "The Letters to Timothy, Titus and Philemon" in *The Daily Study Bible* (Bangalore: Theological, 1999).

[2] Ibid.

[3] "Do Your Best". https://www.ysamphy.com.

[4] Ibid.

for victory, but to do my best."[5] It is about living as fully as one can each passing day.[6]

Attaining self-mastery is a serious struggle that involves engaging one's deep-rooted excesses to conquer them. To succeed, this struggle must be fought well. One needs to give their all in this fight. Debasish Mridha says, "The best way to create a better future is to do your best."[7] There may be a few instances of failure and probably big-time failures in some instances. But a person on the journey towards attaining self-mastery need not allow these instances of failure to discourage him in this struggle. It was William McRaven who once said that "I sometimes fell short of being the best, but I never fell short of giving my best".[8] What is needed is consistency and persistence.

The journey to attain self-mastery requires putting up a good fight, which means doing one’s best. A person embarking on the journey towards attaining self-mastery cannot entertain half measures. It is a struggle to be undertaken with one's whole heart. The struggle requires an honest effort.

---

[5] Ibid.

[6] David Erichsen, “Always Do Your Best and Watch Your Best Get Better". https://www.lifehack.com.

[7] “Do Your Best”. https://www.ysamphy.com.

[8] Ibid.

Chapter 40

THE SCARED LITTLE SELF

"Do not fear, only believe." (Mark 5:36).

Do you recall those days, as a little child, when fear of certain things held you from coming out of your house except when you were with someone like mom or dad or someone you were sure would protect you? For some people, a harmless, rough-mustached teddy bear was enough to give them goose pimples and keep them behind closed doors.

Jacobson enumerates some common childhood fears, such as fear of being alone, the dark, dogs or other big animals, bugs, heights, getting shots or going to the doctor, unfamiliar things, places, or people, loud noises, and imaginary monsters like the "thing" under the bed.[1] Such fears deny some children peace and serve as a source of restriction. For some individuals, the fear can be so severe as to be tormenting. Some parents or guardians cash in on such fears to instill a sense of loyalty and obedience in a child's tender mind.

In life generally, but particularly on the journey towards self-mastery, it is important to know that some people carry their scared little selves with them. Unfortunately, many seem unaware that they carry these childhood fears into adulthood. This mani-

[1] Rae Jacobson. https://childmind.org/.

fests and constitutes a strong drawback when a person wants to take a bold step in life.

The scared little self sometimes manifests as doubts about one's abilities. Most of the time, encouragement from parents, guardians, teachers, and/or mentors helps the child discover his capabilities and conquer his doubts. For instance, to take the first step in walking, a child is overwhelmed by fears and doubts about whether he can walk. It takes the guidance of parents and guardians to help the child overcome that fear. What the parents and guardians do in this circumstance is to give the child courage.

According to Elianna Platt, being afraid sometimes is a normal and healthy part of growing up.[2] She further points out that fear is an inescapable part of being a kid.[3] While some parents, guardians, teachers, and mentors pamper children by presenting themselves as superheroes who always shield them from what they fear, the best approach is to help children overcome their fears.[4]

Carried over to the adult stage of life, some people have doubts about their abilities and capabilities. Whenever they want to explore new things, they have self-doubts about whether what they want to do is the right thing. If they muster the courage to start at all, the same self-doubt accompanies them, asking whether they are doing it the right way, at the right time, and whether what they do will gain people's approval. Such doubts could gradually snowball into perplexity.

---

[2] Ibid.

[3] Ibid.

[4] Ibid.

Such feelings of doubt from the scared little self can make one feel intimidated, leading one either not to start at all or to give up after starting. Most failures in life, and abandoned projects and dreams, are the result of doubts from people's scared little selves, not necessarily of incompetence.

The scared little self makes some people afraid of the embarrassment that comes with failure. Consequently, they will prefer never to make any trial at all. The fear of embarrassment holds some people back from exploring their talents or pursuing them to the highest heights. This kind of fear of failure condemns an individual to a state of naivety.

Criticism is another thing the scared little self tries to avoid. For the little self, criticism means you messed up. But this is not always the case. Honest and constructive criticism is often a challenge to improve. If only one could stand on the scared little self, one would have taken criticism as a stepping stone to self-growth and development by noting the areas pointed out and working on them.

God wishes that we overcome our scared little selves. He admonishes; "Fear not, for I am with you, be not dismayed, for I am your God; I will strengthen you, I will help you, I will uphold you with my victorious right hand" (Isaiah 41:10); "Fear not, for I have redeemed you; I have called you by name, you are mine" (43:1); "Have I not commanded you? Be strong and of good courage; be not frightened, neither be dismayed; for the Lord your God is with you wherever you go" (Joshua 1:9); For I, the Lord your God, hold your right hand; it is I who say to you, 'Fear not, I will help you.' Fear not, you worm Jacob, you men of Israel! I will help you, says the Lord; your Redeemer is the Holy One of Israel" (Isaiah 41:13-14).

The scared little self rubs a person of confidence. It weakens and destroys the courage a person needs to discover and develop their capabilities and accomplish tasks begun. It dwarfs the person's courage so that the person curls back into his shell. A person who has not overcome his scared little self can hardly be considered accomplished. The person would rather stay safe, out of fear of trying, failing, and bearing the shame, disappointment, or hurt.

The journey towards self-mastery can be very challenging, and one's scared little self can rise at one stage or another to frustrate it. In all these, a person embarking on this journey needs to listen to Jesus speak these words always: “Do not fear, only believe” (Mark 5:36). With these words, the person should gain courage and move on. In my personal life and struggle to become a better person, I have listened to Christ's words, and they have always given me the courage to move on.

No one should give up on himself or herself. No matter how much toll one’s weaknesses and excesses have taken on one, things can always get better. I have had my down moments as a priest. One thing, however, that I have been consistent with is that I have never given up on myself but rather have trusted in God’s help. As you read this book, you may feel or know someone who is crippled by their weaknesses and excesses to the point of losing hope in the possibility of attaining any level of self-mastery. Believe me, that is not the end of the story. What a person needs is to make up one’s mind, rise, and try. God will come in, and one will be surprised by the amazing outcome.

Bibliography

Books

The Catechism of the Catholic Church (Nairobi: Pauline, 1994).

Adimonye, Aloysius M. *My Conscience: My Guiding Light* (Enugu: SNAAP, 2002).

Aquinas, Thomas. *Summa Theologiae: A Concise Translation.* McDermott, Timothy (Ed.) (Notre Dame: Christian Classics, 1989).

Attwater, Donald (Edt.). *A Catholic Dictionary* (Third Edition) (Illinois: TAN BOOKS, 19907).

Barclay, William. "The Letters to Timothy, Titus and Philemon" in *The Daily Study Bible* (Bangalore: Theological, 1999).

Barclay, William. *The Daily Study Bible: The Gospel According to Luke* (Bangalore: Theological, 1999). Luke 19:12-26. This is on the parable of the ten gold coins. It is St. Luke's version of Matthew's parable of the talents (Mt 25:14-30). Glenn, Paul J. *A Tour of the Summa of St. Thomas Aquinas* (Bangalore: Theological, 2007).

Glenn, Paul J. *A Tour of the Summa of St. Thomas Aquinas* (Bangalore: Theological, 2007).

Hardon, John A. *Pocket Catholic Dictionary* (New York: IMAGE BOOKS, 1985).

Jone, Heribert. *Moral Theology* (Rockford, IL: TAN, 1993).

Kordell, Jerome. *The Gospel According to Luke* (Mumbai: St Paul, 2001).

Life Application Study Bible (Illinois: Tyndale, 2007).

Macmillan English Dictionary for Advanced Learners (New Edition) (Oxford: Macmillan, 2007).

Macmillan English Dictionary for Advanced Learners. Second Edition (Oxford: Macmillan, 2007).

McBrien, Richard P. (Ed). *The HarperCollins Encyclopedia of Catholicism* (New York: HarperCollins, 1995).

McBrien, Richard. *Catholicism* (London: St. Paul's, 2008).

McCarthy, Flor. *New Sunday and Holyday Liturgies Year C* (Dublin: Dominican, 2000).

Oxford Advanced Learner's Dictionary of Current English (Fourth Edition) (Oxford: Oxford, 1993).

Oxford Advanced Learner's Dictionary, Fourth Edition (Oxford: Oxford, 1993).

Pazhayampallil, Thomas. *Pastoral Guide, Vol. 1* (Bangalore: Kristu Jyoti, 2004).

Peschke, Karl-Heinz. *Christian Ethics: Moral Theology in the Light of Vatican II, Vol. 1* (Bangalore: Theological, 1996).

Peschke, Karl H. *Christian Ethics: Moral Theology in the Light of Vatican II, Vol. II* (Bangalore: Theological, 1996).

Rahner, Karl. "Virtue" in *Encyclopedia of Theology: A Concise Sacramentum Mundi.* Edited by Karl Rahner (Mumbai: St. Paul, 2004).

St. Augustine. *The Confessions* (Part I, vol. 1) (New York: Augustinian Heritage Institute, 1997).

The Holy Bible.

The International Bible Commentary (Bangalore: Theological). Commentary on Matthew 7:1.

Farmer, William R., ed. *The International Bible Commentary* (Bangalore: Theological, 1998).

The International Webster's Comprehensive Dictionary of English Language (Encyclopedic Edition) (Naples, FL: Typhoon International, 2004).

The Oxford Minireference Dictionary (New) (Oxford: Oxford, 1995).

Trese, Leo J. *The Faith Explained* (Lagos: Criterion, 2007).

William Barclay. "The Gospel of Matthew Volume 1". *The Daily Study Bible* (Bangalore: Theological, 1999).

Internet Sources

_ (https//www.partnersinlesdership.com.

_ (https//www.therealpresence.org/archives/Q_and_A/Q_and_A_024.htm.

_ (https://bible.org/seriespage.

_ (https://languages.oup.com/google-dictionary-en/.

_ (https://medium.com/the-logician/stop-with-the-excuses-its-time-to-make-a-change-87990fc6a9d6.

_ (https://punching.com.

_ (https://t.guardian.ng.

_ (https://www.brainyquote.com/quotes/anton_chekhov_119058.

_ (https://www.ghanaweb.com.

_ (https://www.google.com/amp/s/schoolworkhelper.net.

_ (https://www.iep.utm.edu/aris-eth.

_ (https://www.skillsyouneed.com.

_ (https:www.pursuit-of-happiness.org.

_ (www.christianweek.org.
_ (www.dictionary.cambridge.org.
_ (www.gr8tness.com.
_ (www.ldoceonline.com.
_ (www.lexicon.com.
_ (www.newadvent.org.
_ (www.psychologytoday.com.
_ www.usccb.org. Also see Eucharistic Prayer IV.
_ (www.webmd.com.
_ (www.womenontop.com.
_ (https://www.invaji.com/confucius-quotes/.
_ (www.brainyquote.com.
_ (www.dgreetings.com.
_ (www.mindtools.com.
_ (www.brainyquote.com.

"Blame Game Toxic People" https://www.learning-mind.com/blame-game-toxic-people.

"Decision Making Principles" https://www.watermark.org/blog/decision-making-principles.

"Defining Spiritual Wisdom For Yourself" www.everydayhealth.com.

"Do Your Best" (www.ysamphy.com

"Fulfilment" (https://www.google.com/amp/s/www.psychologytoday.com/intl/blog/fulfiillment-any-age/201509.

"Homing" (https://www.dictionary.com/browse/homing.

"How to Fix Bad Decisions" (https://biblestudytools.com/blogs/chris-russell/how-to-fix-bad-decisions.html.

"How to Tame the Terrible Tongue" (www.keepbelieving.com/sermon/how-to-tame-the-terrible-tongue/.

"Instinct as Behaviour" https://www.britannica.com/topic/instinct/instinct-as-behaviour.

"Internal Monologue" (www.en.m.wikipedia.org

"Managing Your Internal Dialogue" (www.skillsyouneed.com.

"Nature Abhors a Vacuum" (https://www.englishclub.com/ref/esl/Sayings/Quizzes/Mixed_2/Nature_abhors_a_vacuum_555.php.

"People Who Blame Others for their Actions" (https://www.google.com/search?q=people%20who%20blame%20others%20for20their%20actions&...

"Pope Warns Against Close-Mindedness of Intellectual Aristocracy" (https://www.catholicnewsagency.com./news/pope-warns-against-close-mindedness-of-intellectual-aristocracy.

"Power of Repetition" (https://getlighthouse.com/blog/power-of-repetition-successful-leaders.

"Pruning in the Bible" (https://www.arynthelibrary.com/pruning -in-the-bible.

"Self-Preservation" Merriam Webster Dictionary (Since 1828) (https://www.merriam-websterdictionary.com/dictionary/self-preservation.

"Self-reproach" https://www.merriam-webster.com/thesaurus/self-reproach.

"St. Augustine of Hippo" https://catholicdos.org.

"The Biblical Way to Overcome Victim Mentality and Be a Victor" (https://folcc.org/the-biblical-way-to-overcome-victim-mentality-and-be-a-victor/)

"The Johari Window Model Theory" (https://communication-theory.org/the-johari-window-model/.

"The Johari Window" (https://www.toppr.com/guides/business-communication-and-ethics/intro-to-business-communication/johari-window/.

"What do You Call Someone Who Blames Others for their Actions?" (https://www.quora.com./What-do-you-call-someone-who-blames-others-for-their-own-actions.

"What Should a Virtuous Person Possess?" (https://poe.com/Sage.

"Will" (https://www.biblestudytools.com/dictionary/will/.

Adamu, John. https://www.brainyquote.com

Akwei, Ismail (https://face2faceafrica.com/article/wwe-star-kofi-kingston-returns-home-to-ghana-after-26-years-hotos.

Atman, Kim. "The Importance of Being 'Principle Centered'" (www.teachingvalues.com.

Balogh, Akos (https://au-thegospelcoalition-org.cdn.ampproject.org/v/s/au.

Bartunek, John (https://catholicexchange.com/occasion-sin-sin.

Bible Works (BibleWorks–[c:\programfiles (x86)\BibleWorks7\init\btw700.swc].

Cambridge Dictionary (https://dictionary.cambrige.org.

Chamberlain H. Guthrie (https://wisdom-trek.com/archive-1/day-116/

Dempsey, Rich (https://econfaculty.gmu.edu/bcaplan/instinct2.

Dreyfuss, Emily (https://www.google.com/amp/s/www.wired.com/2017/02/dont-believe-lies-just-prople-people-repeat/amp.

Erichsen, David. "Always Do Your Best and Watch Your Best Get Better" (www.lifehack.com.

Estes, Marla. "Aloneness and Inner Peace" (https://ashland-tidings.com.

Fatima, Mehak (https://bornrealist.com/self-will/.

Forsdike, Josy. https://www.theguardian.com/us-news/galary/2015/jul/25/.....

Gillian, Seth J. https://www.psychologytoday.com/us/blog/think-act-be/201511....

Hardy Benjamin P. "The Two Mental Shifts Highly Successful People Make" (www.qz.com.

Hardy Benjamin P. The Two Mental Shifts Highly Successful People Make (www.qz.com.

Harrington Daniel J. "Sirach" (15:11-20). The International Bible Commentary: An Ecumenical Commentary For The Twenty-First Century (Bangalore: Theological, 2007).

Herche, Katie. "The Importance of Principles." https://www.principles.org.

Hosie, Rachel. "Is it Possible to Change Your Personality Past the Age of 30?" (www.independent.co.uk.

Ignatius Obinwa. Igbo Proverb (Oral Interview on 05.02.2020).

Internet Encyclopedia of Philosophy (https://iep.utm.edu/epicur/..

Jacob Son, Rae. https://childmind.org/.

Kattalia, Kathryn. "Our Personalities Stop Changing Once We Turn 30, Science Says, But It's Not As Depressing As It Sounds" https://www.bustle.com.

Lamb, Robert. “Power of the Will” https://science.howstuffworks.com/life/inside-the-mind-/human-brain/willpowe3.htm.

Merriam-Webster Dictionary (https://www.merriam-webster.com.

Moore, Anthony (www.medium.com.

Pope Francis. *Gaudete et Exsultate* (https://www.vatican.va.

Pope Paul VI. *Gravissimum Educationis* (www.vatican.va)

Ritenbaugh, John W. “What the Bible Says About Self Mastery” (https://bibletools.org/index.cfm/fuseaction/Topical.show/RTD/cgg/ID/136Self-Mastery.htm.

Sasson, Remez. (https://www.successconsciousness.com/index_00004b.htm.

Shaw, Victor N. "Self-Dialogue as a Fundamental Process of Expression" in *JSTOR* (https://www.jstor.org.

Smith, Richard H. (www.psychologytoday.com.

Wiktionary (https://en.m.wiktionary.org.

Winter, Saysi (www.quora.com.

Other Sources

Nnamene C. Everistus. Make Your Choice. (Homily delivered at the St. John the Baptist Chaplaincy, CIWA, Obehie), early February 2020.

Very Rev. Fr. Ibrahim Bawa Yakubu (Quote sent via WhatsApp on 08.02.2021).

Banta, Swandy (Phone conversation on 15.01.2021).

www.ingramcontent.com/pod-product-compliance
Lightning Source LLC
LaVergne TN
LVHW040219110826
845146LV00005B/1345

* 9 7 9 8 8 8 8 7 0 4 4 2 4 *